Drawing in the Digital Age

Drawing in the Digital Age

AN OBSERVATIONAL METHOD FOR ARTISTS AND ANIMATORS

WEI XU, PHD

WILEY

John Wiley & Sons, Inc.

Acquisitions Editor: Mariann Barsolo
Development Editor: Gary Schwartz
Technical Editor: James Haldy
Production Editor: Eric Charbonneau
Copy Editor: Sharon Wilkey
Editorial Manager: Pete Gaughan
Production Manager: Tim Tate
Vice President and Executive Group Publisher: Richard Swadley
Vice President and Publisher: Neil Edde
Book Designer: Caryl Gorska
Compositor: Maureen Forys, Happenstance Type-O-Rama
Proofreader: Kim Wimpsett
Indexer: Ted Laux
Project Coordinator, Cover: Katherine Crocker
Cover Designer: Ryan Sneed
Cover Images: Wei Xu, PhD

Copyright © 2012 by John Wiley & Sons, Inc., Indianapolis, Indiana

Published simultaneously in Canada

ISBN: 978-1-118-17650-4 (pbk.)
ISBN: 978-1-118-22716-9 (ebk)
ISBN: 978-1-118-23315-3 (ebk)
ISBN: 978-1-118-26479-9 (ebk)

For general information on our other products and services or to obtain technical support, please contact our Customer Care Department within the U.S. at (877) 762-2974, outside the U.S. at (317) 572-3993 or fax (317) 572-4002.

Wiley also publishes its books in a variety of electronic formats and by print-on-demand. Not all content that is available in standard print versions of this book may appear or be packaged in all book formats. If you have purchased a version of this book that did not include media that is referenced by or accompanies a standard print version, you may request this media by visiting http://booksupport.wiley.com. For more information about Wiley products, visit us at www.wiley.com.

Library of Congress Control Number: 2011945578

10 9 8 7 6 5 4 3 2 1

Dear Reader,

Thank you for choosing *Drawing in the Digital Age: An Observational Method for Artists and Animators*. This book is part of a family of premium-quality Sybex books, all of which are written by outstanding authors who combine practical experience with a gift for teaching.

Sybex was founded in 1976. More than 30 years later, we're still committed to producing consistently exceptional books. With each of our titles, we're working hard to set a new standard for the industry. From the paper we print on to the authors we work with, our goal is to bring you the best books available.

I hope you see all that reflected in these pages. I'd be very interested to hear your comments and get your feedback on how we're doing. Feel free to let me know what you think about this or any other Sybex book by sending me an email at nedde@wiley.com. If you think you've found a technical error in this book, please visit http://sybex.custhelp.com. Customer feedback is critical to our efforts at Sybex.

Best regards,

Neil Edde
Vice President and Publisher
Sybex, an Imprint of Wiley

*To my parents
and family*

Acknowledgments

First and foremost, I would like to thank my parents for fostering my artistic dreams when I was a little child. This book originated from those small dreams.

I am grateful to my wife, Lin, for her continuous support for this book project.

Thanks also go to my lovely daughter, Alicia, and my clever son, Daniel, for being the first users of the new method I describe in this book. Their initial learning success validated that my method is easy to learn, and even kids can pick it up without difficulty.

I offer profound thanks to the wonderful team at Wiley, especially Mariann Barsolo and Jenni Housh for establishing the book project and working on the contract quickly, Gary Schwartz for polishing my scripts as well as turning my "Chinenglish" into English, James Haldy for spotting and fixing technical issues, Pete Gaughan for solving template issues, and Eric Charbonneau for making the book ready for publication. Also contributing to the book you now hold were copy editor Sharon Wilkey, proofreader Kim Wimpsett, and compositor Maureen Forys. Thanks again to all for a job exceptionally well done.

This book is the product of years of research and art learning. I'd like to thank members of the faculty and staff of the Art Institute of California at San Diego for their assistance in my art education and writing about art, particularly the following individuals (in alphabetical order): Jack Beduhn, Christian Bradley, Rebecca Browning, Dr. Alicia Butters, Elizabeth Erickson, Harry Hamernik, Jason Katsoff, Wattana Khommarath, Jack Madi, Dr. Mary McDermott, Dzu Nguyen, Lena Pham, Grace Piano, Dr. Kim Varey, and Grady Williams.

I also want to thank the students at the Art Institute of California at San Diego for attending my workshops and giving me positive feedback over the past two years. Without their involvement, my method could still be in the research stage instead of being a published book. Special thanks go to my students Alvin Revilas and Blake Fox for their proofreading of my research articles related to this book.

Of course, I cannot forget to thank Susan Varnum, Dr. Edward Abeyta, and Robin Wittman of the University of California San Diego Extension for their efforts to set up a new art class to teach my method in the winter of 2012.

I owe debts of gratitude to faculty, staff, and students at Zhejiang University, especially Dr. Weidong Geng and Ms. Xiao Li for inviting me to lecture their multimedia students on my drawing method in the summer of 2011.

I'd like to thank Alex Reed for her language assistance in preparing the first draft of this book.

Finally, I want to thank you, the reader, for picking up this book and taking an exciting drawing journey with me!

About the Author

 *Wei Xu, PhD,* is a computer scientist, mathematician, and artist. Currently, he serves as faculty or adjunct/ visiting faculty at several universities including the Art Institute of California at San Diego, the University of California San Diego Extension, and Zhejiang University (China). He is also the president and cofounder of Geomy Entertainment, a video game consulting and mobile app development firm.

Being a computer scientist and video game veteran, Dr. Xu offers a wide range of video game production classes for college students and technical training for game companies. As an artist, he has been hosting drawing workshops at the Art Institute of California at San Diego since 2009. Starting January 2012, he will officially offer drawing classes to teach his new drawing system, the ABC method, at both the Art Institute of California at San Diego and the University of California San Diego Extension.

Dr. Xu obtained his doctoral degree in computer graphics and applied mathematics from the University of Texas at Austin. He also holds an MS degree in applied math and computer graphics from ZheJiang University, China, and a BS in computational mathematics from Fudan University, China. He has served as the lead engineer for game technology R&D at Sony Computer Entertainment America, San Diego. Prior to joining Sony, he was a senior computer graphics software engineer at the Schlumberger Austin Technology Center.

CONTENTS AT A GLANCE

Contents

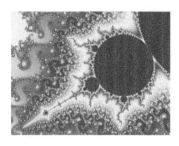

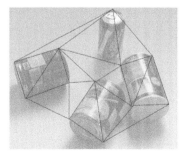

Introduction

Why I Wrote This Book

Up until five years ago, I honestly had never thought about writing an art book in my entire life. As a mathematician and computer graphics scientist, it seemed that I should have a million reasons to write a 3D math or mobile-game programming book before I would even think about writing a book about drawing. Also, you would not have expected a drawing book to be written by a person who does not have an official art degree. But everything has its explainable and logical reasons.

My Lost Dream

I was born and raised in a small town on the east coast of China. Because the region was so underdeveloped, I did not have a chance to get any art training beyond the school's limited art classes when I was a child. After entering middle school, I received some special attention from my school's art teacher. He taught me the grid method—a fancy method I had never used before. I was immediately addicted to this "magic" method because my drawing improved in no time. I practiced it a lot, until a year later when I sadly learned that I couldn't draw anything without a grid! With my mother's advice, I stopped using the method immediately, but it still took me more than a year to recover my freehand drawing skill. Learning the wrong drawing method was a big lesson! I considered myself a self-taught amateur because most of my time after that incident was spent on drawing without instruction. Becoming an artist was my dream since childhood, but the dream never materialized in China. When I graduated from high school, I couldn't go to any art school because of their extremely limited enrollment size. Instead, I ended up as a math major at Fudan University, a top university in China known for its math education department. Eventually, I became a mathematician and computer graphics scientist after graduate studies in both China and the United States. I rarely drew after I started college, and my artistic dream was set aside for many years.

In 2005, however, my dream was reignited when I joined the faculty for video game education at the Art Institute of California at San Diego. Being situated in an art environment, I found many opportunities to learn art in my spare time. When I picked up learning art again after so many years of abandon, I suddenly discovered that art is very close to math—a fact commonly ignored. In fact, art is separated from math and science in education systems worldwide. In my opinion, drawing is an engineering process involving the arrangement of geometric shapes, and math is the best tool for helping us to draw.

Certainly, my professional math and computer graphics background allowed me to apply mathematical theories and scientific principles to my drawing. My experience inspired me to carry out a serious personal research project on bringing math and computer graphics principles into drawing. The research progressed slowly in my spare time. However, it became clear to me that graphical information could be extracted and duplicated on paper with basic math knowledge. In this way, drawing is both more learnable and teachable because every step has a clear instruction and goal. Thus I had a strong desire to teach drawing in a new, scientific way.

An Easy and Constructive Method

In 2007, I began to test the waters by teaching this new drawing method (later called the *ABC method*) to my own kids as an after-school project. Although this method was not mature at that time, teaching it to my children helped me improve it a lot. Because every step is explainable in this new method, my kids didn't have much trouble learning it.

The results were very promising. Figure I.1 is a collection of pencil drawings done by my 13-year-old daughter after two years of practicing with me. Figure I.2 shows some of my son's drawing samples when he had just turned 7. He did a very good job in controlling proportions, even though he understood very little about geometry. I was very glad that my new method could be taught to children. If a kid can learn the method, then it should be easy for adults.

Encouraged by the success of teaching my children, I wanted to expand the teaching of the method to a broader audience including professional art students—even though math knowledge was not emphasized in the typical art curriculum. Meanwhile, art students frequently requested that I demonstrate my math tricks to them to improve their drawing efficiency. In 2009, I started offering a series of workshops on "Life Drawing Efficiently with Mathematics" at the Art Institute of California at San Diego. The workshops have never stopped since then, and now the ABC drawing method is part of the video game students' curriculum.

Figure I.1

My 13-year old daughter's pencil drawing after two years of practice with the ABC method

Drawing by Alicia (age 13)

After two years of workshops teaching professional art students the applications of math in art, I introduced my nonconventional method at two international art conferences in early 2011. The purpose was to raise awareness about the benefits of integrating math and art in teaching art students draftsmanship skills.

The art community has been dominated by right-brain theory for a long time, and math knowledge was critically missing in art education. As a consequence, many artists cannot execute a basic drawing and lack a systematic approach to arranging shapes. Many art books still teach students often outdated drawing methods that do not have any scientific support, and some even work against scientific principles. Looking back in art history, math and art used to be integrated during the Renaissance, and it generated some great artists who were also mathematicians or engineers. Da Vinci and Michelangelo are probably the best well-known examples. But what is the situation today? Why did we take a step backward by dropping math knowledge in art education?

- Two major components in the drawing process, and how they are closely related to math

- Why we should take a full-brain approach to drawing instead of a right-brain-only approach, and the current status of using math in existing drawing methods

- How an object is structured, and the kind of spatial properties that shapes have

- How 2D and 3D objects can be unified so that we can approach them with the same method

- How various graphical structures are used to help us draw objects, and how to extract them with triangulation

- The criteria for designing a good drawing method

- Six basic drawing techniques you should master, and how the ABC method works based on these techniques

Various additional techniques—along with demonstrations designed to teach you how to draw objects from the simple to the complex, from single objects to a group of objects, and from a still life to a quick sketch—are taught throughout this book. All of these techniques are designed to take full advantage of the geometric properties of objects. These techniques include how to select key points, how to use reference lines, how to group graphical structures, how to use a hierarchical approach, how to create virtual skeletons, how to use curved triangles and polygons, and how to draw a group of ovals quickly.

Drawing Materials Needed in This Book

The materials used for black-and-white, nonrendering drawing in this book are quite simple:

- *Pencils:* Both mechanical and traditional lead pencils are fine. I recommend mechanical pencils because you don't need to render the drawing, and you can avoid sharpening pencils frequently.

- *Drawing paper:* Any drawing paper works. Beginners may try small sizes such as 9″ × 12″ and gradually move to larger sizes, say, 14″ × 17″ or 18″ × 24″, as your skills advance.

- *Drawing board:* I strongly suggest a drawing board, as shown in Figure I.3. The board enables you to easily hold paper vertically, by placing the board either in an easel or against a chair back.

- *Erasers:* Either regular stationery erasers or professional kneaded erasers are okay. Although discouraged, using a eraser is still required occasionally.

- *Tools:* Absolutely *no* rulers or any other measurement tools are needed to complete the exercises in this book. Even if you have used them in the past, it is a good idea to abandon them now to learn to draw efficiently.

Figure I.3

Drawing pad, papers, and pencils

How to Use This Book

This book contains two parts: theory and practice. Chapters 1 to 3 form the theory component, while Chapters 4 to 8 are for practice. The entire book is designed to present a set of new theories and corresponding techniques in sequential order. Thus, it is strongly recommended that you read all chapters in numerical sequence without jumping around.

The demonstrations and exercises in this book are designed to go from easy to hard so that you can learn progressively. Please take your time to read the text content, follow the demonstrations, and do the exercises in each chapter. Remember that it is not enough to just learn the theory—you have to apply the theories and increase your drawing skill through practice.

Chapters 1–3 cover the supporting theory behind this book. Chapter 1 explains why art is closely related to math and how math can help in learning art. An observational drawing process is viewed as two parts: extracting shapes from a scene and managing these shapes on paper. Existing drawing methods and their connection to math are also analyzed.

The main topic of Chapter 2 is how to extract graphical structures from a scene by using basic geometry theories and modern computer graphics principles. The chapter explains how an object is structured and also the spatial properties of shapes. The major technical terms employed in this book are introduced in this chapter.

Chapter 3 discusses the criteria for a good drawing method followed by the introduction of the new scientific method, which is at the core of this book. The new method is divided into six basic skills, and each of them is closely related to the concept of angles. Demonstrations are provided to show you how the method works for various subjects.

Chapters 4–8 introduce various special techniques accompanied by step-by-step demonstrations to help you draw with the ABC method. Each chapter includes its own exercises to reinforce the topic covered in that particular chapter. It is strongly suggested that all exercises be completed before going on to the next chapter because of the dependency of the content.

Chapter 4 teaches you how to draw simple objects with the ABC method. Then, in Chapter 5, additional techniques covering how to draw complicated objects are presented. After that, Chapter 6 talks about how to draw a scene consisting of multiple objects.

Chapters 7 and 8 introduce some advanced techniques. Chapter 7 introduces curved triangles/polygons to improve the efficiency of the ABC method further, while Chapter 8 talks about the various techniques needed to draw human beings. Topics include how to draw people, how to draw faces, and how to draw quick life figures.

Pretest

It is important to ensure that you improve your drawing ability by the time you finish this book, whether you use it as a textbook for an art class or as a self-teaching tool. One simple way to verify your progress is to record your current drawing level now so that you have a reference for comparison in the future. Thus, before you start reading Chapter 1, please take the following pretest.

Draw the picture shown in Figure I.4 on a regular sheet of paper (8.5″ × 11″ or larger). During this pretest, only free-hand drawing is allowed—you are not allowed to use any tools or tool-assisted methods, such as the grid method. Give yourself enough time to do your best work, but you should not take any longer than 4 hours. Do not rush, because drawing accurately is more important than speed here. After you finish, on the back of the paper write down the date and the time it took you to complete the drawing. Keep the drawing in a safe place or make a digital copy. You will need it to evaluate your progress when you are finished with this book.

The figure you were asked to draw is a pencil drawing of Van Gogh's self-portrait. I made this line-drawing version from Van Gogh's original oil painting, so it should be much easier for you than drawing from the original lineless painting.

One major goal of this book is to help you learn how to draw more efficiently by applying math and scientific principles. It is probably also why you purchased this book instead of all the others available. Nothing will give you more joy than seeing your drawing skills improve in a short period of time. I've observed great delight among the students who attended my lectures or workshops in the past, and I hope you will have similar, exciting results.

PRETEST WITH 3D SCENES

Obviously, observational drawing is more about drawing real 3D scenes than copying 2D artwork. However, because of the limitation of working with a printed book page, I am unable to set a 3D scene before you. Additionally, you need to draw something complicated in this pretest. By tackling a hard task now, it will be easier to judge your progress later, and that is why I selected the Van Gogh portrait.

If you'd prefer to track your skills by drawing a 3D object, please feel free to do so. Make sure you can re-create the same scene when needed in order to draw it again in the near future.

Figure I.4

Image for the pretest

How to Contact the Author

I welcome feedback from you about this book or about books you'd like to see from me in the future. You can reach me by writing to Wei Xu at artBook@geomy.com. For more information about my work, please visit my Facebook page at

www.facebook.com/DrawScientifically

Sybex strives to keep you supplied with the latest tools and information you need for your work. Please check their website at www.sybex.com/go/drawing, where we'll post additional content and updates that supplement this book if the need arises.

CHAPTER 1

Understanding the Relationship between Math and Art

After a certain high level of technical skill is achieved, science and art tend to coalesce in esthetics, plasticity, and form. —ALBERT EINSTEIN (1879–1955), SCIENTIST AND ARTIST

Math and fine art (or simply art) are two of the most interesting subjects to explore. However, their relationship may seem paradoxical. Unlike the bond of math and science, the association between math and art is not so obvious. The average person might have difficulty seeing any direct connection between math and art because of their distinct content and methodologies. Instead, the strict logic used in math and the emotional expressions portrayed in art might make the two subjects seem like polar opposites. Yet some experts think otherwise.

So, what is the truth? What are the differences and similarities between math and art? Are they really linked in any sense? If yes, how do they affect and help each other? This chapter provides answers to these questions. In order to lay the foundation for later introducing a new method of learning art, this chapter also focuses on the following topics:

- Ways that math can be used to help us learn about art

- Existing drawing methods and their connections with math

- Reasons that separating math from art is a serious mistake

Understanding How Math and Art Differ

Art and math are indeed very different in at least the following two aspects:

- In terms of content, math is an abstraction of patterns, whereas art is a visual product that provides aesthetic value.

- In terms of methodology, we must process everything in math sequentially by strictly following logic and proven rules. In art, the way we create and learn is subjective and empirical.

Differences in Content

Math and art exhibit distinct differences in their content. Math is the study of numbers, properties, and the relationships of quantities. Either a research paper or a student exercise (later referred to as "math work") tries to show that some quantity patterns exist in a particular problem. Although math is abstract, it comes from and applies to almost everything: science, technology, economics, and even art.

Mathematics and Culture I, edited by Michele Emmer (Springer-Verlag, 2004), details some of these interconnections between math and other disciplines.

Art is a visual product that displays graphics appealing to an audience and the artist. An artwork may originate from real scenes, but it is most influenced by the artist's emotions and senses.

A math work involves a sequence of logic operations that delivers results by using theories, symbols, and established procedures. Math concepts may be fully abstract and imaginary, as they are not necessarily associated with any real objects in the physical world. Such abstractness allows math to be used as a language to describe and solve problems in science and engineering. Math integrates a strong sense of correct or incorrect. Its content is objective—that is, a math work has the same meaning across all cultures at all times. The purpose of math work is either to develop a new theory for future use or to solve a problem based on existing theories. In math circles, a new math research article is accepted only if it presents new results and is proven to be correct by experts. Otherwise, showing the article to the public would be almost meaningless, even if the work were done by a famous mathematician.

In contrast, a piece of artwork, either two-dimensional (2D) or three-dimensional (3D), presents visual structures that express an artist's thoughts or represent objects the artist observed or imagined. By using shapes, colors, textures, and patterns, artists intend to communicate with viewers in a graphic language that is easy to understand. Artwork is subjective. Generally speaking, the content carries no sense of right or wrong, provided that the artwork does not go against its cultural standard. Any work completed by an artist can be exhibited to the public as long as the artist is satisfied with the product. Visitors in an art gallery can be quickly drawn into imaginary worlds presented by artists. These viewers have emotional reactions to a painting or object based on their individual experiences that they associate with the contents of the artwork. Artwork will never provide everyone with the same experience because its meaning is rooted deeply in each viewer's culture and personal history.

Differences in Methodologies

The methodologies used in math and art are quite different too. In math, every step has to be processed sequentially by following logic and proven theories without emotion. Although mathematicians may use their wildest imaginations when solving a problem or coming up with a new concept, all of their thoughts must rely on reasoning and proven results. After a problem is solved or a new theory is conceived, the outcome then becomes a stepping-stone for future work, and the best approach to achieve such results may be standardized for others' use. This procedural mechanism makes math easy to learn.

For a math problem, even when there are multiple ways to solve it, the correct answer will be the same no matter which method you use. The key to learning math is to understand its theories and related processes. A math work is about definitions, principles, and logic operations. After the process is understood, anyone can duplicate the entire work perfectly without errors—but without understanding, you could easily get stuck at any step. That is why most of us can master basic math knowledge and operations in school.

Figure 1.1 shows a simple algebra problem—solving a quadratic equation—that can be worked out in two ways. The first method turns the equation into a special form so that the square root can be removed in order to solve the problem. The process requires careful manipulation of the numbers. A mistake at any point would result in a wrong answer. However, mathematicians have already articulated these tedious steps and come up with a standard formula for solving any quadratic equation. The second method involves applying that formula directly, resulting in fewer steps and therefore less hassle.

Figure 1.1

An example of a math problem solved in two ways

Solve $x^2 + x - 1 = 0$

Method #1:

$$x^2 + x + \frac{1}{4} - \frac{5}{4} = 0$$

$$(x + \frac{1}{2})^2 = \frac{5}{4}$$

$$x + \frac{1}{2} = \pm\sqrt{\frac{5}{4}} = \pm\frac{\sqrt{5}}{2}$$

$$x = \frac{-1 \pm \sqrt{5}}{2}$$

Method #2 (using formula):

$$x = \frac{-1 \pm \sqrt{1^2 - 4 \times 1 \times (-1)}}{2 \times 1}$$

$$= \frac{-1 \pm \sqrt{5}}{2}$$

In contrast, the method we use to study and create art is subjective and experimental. The process of creating art is affected by the artist's opinions on the topics and that individual's skills in using particular art tools; thus, artwork is hard to reproduce exactly. Although students are taught theories and principles in art class, in order to turn the theories into real skills, students have to spend most of their time doing hands-on exercises to apply those theories and to master the actual skills of using pens, brushes, and other media. Because of human physical limitations, no one can draw a perfect line or circle, let alone a complicated object, even if the drawing principles are understood. Figure 1.2 shows an observational drawing exercise. Although it is quite simple, drawing the object perfectly is extremely hard, even for experienced artists. In creating a piece of art, artists rely more on emotion, incidental decisions, and skill than theories to lay out graphic components.

Figure 1.2

An example of a basic drawing exercise

Unless duplicating an existing object, artists have a lot of freedom to manipulate contents by all available means. Because of artists' diverse approaches and the lack of standardized processes, it is tough for art students to acquire the methods by which other artists create masterpieces. It is almost impossible, even for the artists themselves, to reproduce their existing work exactly. Meanwhile, the lack of restrictions in creating content allows everyone to produce "artwork" without requiring any formal approval. Learning how to create art does take substantial practice, as it is a hands-on activity. Artists with various levels of skills can sit together to draw the same object and repeat such basic exercises again and again. You will never witness such phenomena when learning math, where you must master lower-level knowledge before learning the higher level. A math professional may never need to practice a basic math operation after it has been mastered.

The strange relationship between creativity and art skills contributes to the poor results of art education in our society. A good art skill does not guarantee a good job in creating artwork. To create an artwork, imagination is more important than skills. You may find some artworks in exhibitions are not different from a work done by a novice. For this reason, many students studying art emphasize expression and imagination more than basic hands-on skills. As a result, even though most adults have spent some time in art classes in elementary and secondary school, they still haven't truly mastered the basic skills.

Understanding How Math and Art Are Similar

Some experts claim that math and art are similar and profoundly connected despite their noticeable differences. For example, the Greek philosopher and scientist Aristotle

(384 BC–322 BC) said, "The mathematical sciences particularly exhibit order, symmetry, and limitation; and these are the greatest forms of the beautiful."

Russian painter Wassily Kandinsky (1866–1944) claimed, "The final abstract expression of every art is number."

Many scholars today draw similar conclusions. In a February 2005 article in *Math Horizons* magazine, Carla Farsi et al. also pointed out that both math and art are creative and share beauty. Although art is traditionally considered a creative activity, the imagination evident in math can be easily proven by the massive production of research work published every year. Such abstract theories, not necessarily linked with real objects or phenomena, cannot be completed without innovative minds. A typical procedure used to develop a new math theory is first to predict a possible result and then provide a logical proof. Obtaining such theoretical outcomes normally needs both professional training and inventive thinking.

Mathematicians strongly agree that math procedures and results exhibited by clean formulas and nice patterns such as repetition, symmetry, uniformity, parallelism, and orthogonality are a matter of "beauty." Even math topics that appear chaotic may well have very structured and neat features. For instance, consider the mathematical constant pi (π), which indicates the ratio of any circle's circumference to its diameter. Usually represented as 3.14, π is actually an irrational number, which means that its decimal digits never end and never repeat in any pattern and that the value seems to be unpredictable. However, mathematicians have already proved that π can be expressed in various "beautiful" formulas, including the following *Madhava-Leibniz series*, which can be found in many math textbooks:

$$\pi = 4 \left(1/1 - 1/3 + 1/5 - 1/7 + 1/9 - 1/11 + \ldots \right)$$

Such phenomenon can also be seen in *probability theory*, which tells us various systematic and predicable outcomes about random events. The Gaussian distribution, nicknamed the *bell curve* based on its shape, is one good example of the certainty of uncertain numbers. The beauty of math is also used as a tool to detect possible mistakes by mathematicians because correct answers and processes tend to be neat and clean. Certainly, mathematicians enjoy such "abstract beauty," just as artists love the visual pleasure in their artwork.

GAUSSIAN DISTRIBUTION OR BELL CURVE

Gaussian distribution is a math model that describes random variables. German great mathematician Carl Friedrich Gauss discovered this distribution in 1809. Many things in nature, such as human ages and heights, are distributed in a bell curve; Gaussian distribution is considered the most important distribution model in statistics.

Math in Art

Math can be found in art in several areas. Artists may intentionally or unintentionally use special math knowledge in their artwork. In addition, math is about hidden patterns in almost everything, including visual and aesthetic features. Math embedded in art is a huge topic, but here I'll briefly show you some obvious examples.

Math Numbers Used in Art

There are quite a few well-known irrational numbers, or *math constants*, that have unusual meanings: φ (≈1.61803), π (≈3.14159), e (≈2.71828), and so on. These numbers exist in calculations and formulas across a wide range of mathematics fields.

According to math history books, the ancient Egyptians and Greeks discovered the *golden ratio* (φ) and found that it generated pleasing results. This interesting number was used in building the Great Pyramids and other architectural wonders. Figure 1.3 shows the golden ratio embedded in the Egyptian Great Pyramid.

GOLDEN RATIO

Assume you have two numbers, a and b. They form a golden ratio if "a+b is to a as a is to b," i.e., (a+b)/a = a/b. This relationship holds only when a/b = φ (≈1.61803).

Figure 1.3

Golden ratio in the Great Pyramid

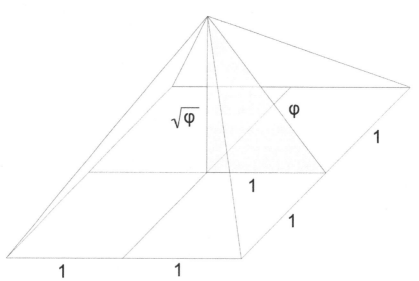

SOURCE: REPRODUCED BY THE AUTHOR FROM *SQUARING THE CIRCLE: GEOMETRY IN ART AND ARCHITECTURE* BY PAUL CALTER (WILEY, 2008).

The *Fibonacci sequence* demonstrates another excellent example of beauty in numbers. The sequence starts from 0 and 1. All other numbers are the sum of the previous two numbers: 0, 1, 1, 2, 3, 5, 8, 13…. The sequence has been proven to be intimately related to the golden ratio. The structures of trees, flowers, and even snail shells can be represented by Fibonacci numbers, which abstract a widely existing pattern in nature in general.

> Many books, including *Lindenmayer Systems, Fractals, and Plants* by Przemyslaw Prusinkiewicz et al. (Springer, 1989), further explore Fibonacci numbers in the nature.

Figure 1.4

Fibonacci structures found in *Mona Lisa*

Some researchers have indicated that the Fibonacci sequence and associated Fibonacci spiral are hidden in the famous painting *Mona Lisa* by Leonardo da Vinci (1452–1511), shown in Figure 1.4. However, not everyone agrees with these findings because da Vinci did not describe such a configuration in his writings. Whether the suggestion is true or not, it is fairly certain that the golden ratio was widely used for composition in many masterpieces because the ratio provides visual harmony. For example, we can find such a "coincidence" in Michelangelo's painting *The creation of Adam*, in which the two fingertips partition the whole painting roughly at 1:1.618 in both horizontal and vertical directions, as indicated in Figure 1.5.

Geometry Used in Art

Geometry is a branch of math that originated from measuring distances in ancient Egyptian land surveys. Over the past thousands of years, geometry has been used almost everywhere, from the sciences to art to our everyday lives. The fundamental concepts such as points, lines, curves, and polygons used in elementary geometry are automatically connected to visual art. Graphic patterns and structures contained in geometric shapes are of artistic value.

Figure 1.5

The golden ratio used for composition

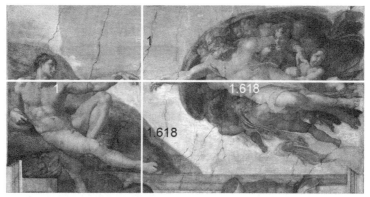

SOURCE: THIS IMAGE IS AVAILABLE AT http://upload.wikimedia.org/wikipedia/commons/0/0c/
Creation_of_Adam_Michelangelo.jpg.

Some special shapes, such as circles, squares, and triangles, are so precious that they serve as fundamental elements in art. For instance, a star is one of the most beautiful geometric shapes in graphic design, and it is used in many national and regional flags (see Figure 1.6).

Figure 1.6

Stars used in flag design

As the ancient Greek tragedian Euripides (480 BC–406 BC) said, "Mighty is geometry; joined with art, resistless."

Artists have used geometry in various ways to create their artwork. You can easily find geometric patterns used explicitly in abstract artwork created by many great artists such as Wassily Kandinsky (1866–1944) and Pablo Picasso (1881–1973).

Dutch graphic artist M.C. Escher (1898–1972) is also well known for his elegant use of geometry in art. He used geometric elements and various styles of symmetries to create unique images that are fascinating to viewers. Some graphic configurations in his artwork are technically impossible in the physical world. Besides using well-designed graphic figures, he also applied math transformations to generate smooth transactions between different shapes.

MATH TRANSFORMATION

Loosely speaking, a math transformation is a math function that turns one image into a new look. Some popular and simple examples are translation, rotation, reflection, and scaling.

Although Escher was not a mathematician, he conducted his own math research for creating artwork, according to Doris Schattschneider in the June/July 2004 issue of the magazine *Notices of the American Mathematical Society*. Using math transforms is an efficient way to create interesting images. Typically, we can start with a simple pattern and then duplicate it with different rotations and scaling to obtain a new pattern. Repeating this process a couple of times will immediately generate a complicated geometric pattern. Figure 1.7 shows one of such examples.

Figure 1.7

A geometric pattern

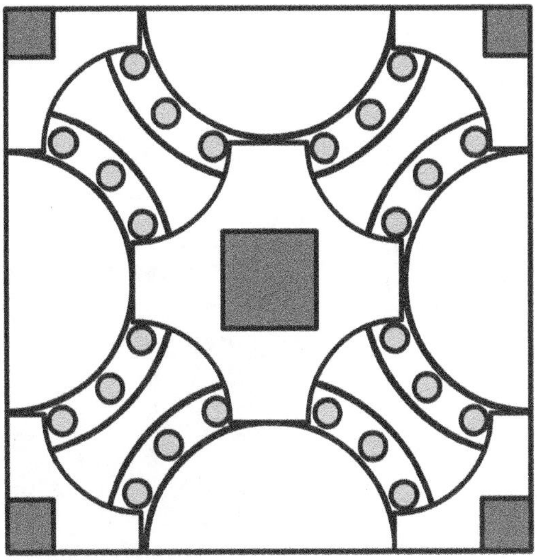

Math Processes Used in Art

In observational drawing, artists usually simplify regular objects into spheres, cylinders, cones, cubes, or combinations of these basic forms. When sketching these geometric structures on paper, they need a careful consideration of the spatial relationship among the objects. These activities are actually forms of math. Figure 1.8 is a sample of an observational drawing in which the artist tried to make sure that every object has its correct location, orientation, and connection with the rest of the scene by performing a 3D analysis. Hidden lines and section curves are drawn to describe spatial features of objects. Parallel lines are sketched to confirm the perspective in the drawing.

Drawing realistically also requires a math operation for projecting an object from 3D space onto paper. This process, known as *perspective transform*, is the core of perspective theory. Officially established in the Renaissance, this theory became a fundamental principle that guides artists in drawing what they observe. You'll learn more details about this theory later in this chapter. For now, Figure 1.9 shows one famous example of the application of the theory: the oil painting *Last Supper* by da Vinci. The ceiling of the room is formed from angled lines that clearly create the illusion of a 3D perspective, as shown by the white lines.

Figure 1.8

Figure 1.8

3D structures in an observational drawing

Figure 1.9

Perspective view in the *Last Supper*

THIS IMAGE IS GENERATED BY THE AUTHOR, BUT *LAST SUPPER* IS AVAILABLE AT http://en.wikipedia.org/wiki/File: Leonardo_da_Vinci_(1452-1519)_-_The_Last_Supper_(1495-1498).jpg.

Art in Math

Although generally most mathematicians are not artists, they often get inspiration from art in their research. To solve problems involved in multiple variables and unknowns, imagining and thinking visually are useful ways for a mathematician to "see" undiscovered patterns. At the same time, modern computers provide a powerful tool to visualize complicated data artistically.

Visual Assistance for Math Work

A math problem is usually very abstract, but it doesn't have to stay that way. Using visual assistance is common in math research. The proof of the Pythagorean theorem and the use of Bézier curves in computer graphics (CG) are good examples.

One of the most famous math discoveries, the Pythagorean theorem, was named for the Greek mathematician Pythagoras (570 BC–495 BC). The theorem unveils a "magical" pattern existing in all right triangles: the square of the length of the hypotenuse (the side opposite the right angle) is always equal to the sum of the squares of the lengths of the other two sides.

After its discovery, mathematicians found several neat ways to prove the theorem. One of them, shown in Figure 1.10, is a visual approach. By tiling four copies of a right triangle together to form a larger square, that square's area is the sum of the areas of those four triangles and the small square in the middle. This simple fact results in the theorem:

$$c^2 = 4 \times 0.5ab + (b - a)2$$
$$c^2 = a^2 + b^2$$

Bézier curves are a perfect example of the mixture of math and art. Named after French engineer and mathematician Pierre Bézier (1910–1999) for his popularizing of this method, Bézier curves have a beautiful graphical structure and can be generated efficiently in computers using following so-called subdivision method. The left image in Figure 1.11 demonstrates this method for a simple case of a cubic Bézier curve determined by four given points: P_0, P_1, P_2, and P_3. The curve is defined as the following math equation:

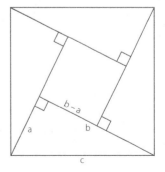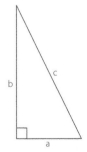

Figure 1.10

Graphic proof of the Pythagorean theorem

$$P(t) = (1 - t)^3P_0 + 3(1 - t)^2tP_1 + 3(1 - t)^2tP_2 + t^3P_3, \text{ for } 0 \le t \le 1.$$

P(t) represents the position of the curve at any particular t – an internal variable that describes the curve. For example, t=0 stands for the starting point, t=1 is the end point, and t=0.5 can be consider the middle point.

The previous math expression may appear scary to many artists, but its construction process is intuitive and stunningly simple. The pyramidal diagram on the right side of Figure 1.11 shows how the value P(t) is obtained step-by-step. For example, point $Q_0 = (1 - t)P_0 + tP_0$ is a weighted average of points P_0 and P_1, and therefore Q_0 is on the line segment $P_0 P_1$. The rest of the vertices in the diagram can be found exactly the same way.

Because of their simplicity and elegance, Bézier curves serve as the industry standard to create curves in today's graphics software programs, such as Adobe Creative Suite (CS) and Autodesk Maya.

Figure 1.11

Bézier curve construction (left) and vertex dependency (right)

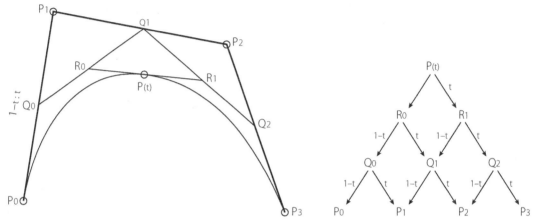

Visualization of Math

In computer technology, color is represented numerically by red, green, and blue components. This allows us to turn an array of numbers into a full screen of colorful dots through visualization techniques. An application of modern CG, *computer visualization* is extremely useful in the sciences and engineering, in which massive numerical information needs to be explored. When numbers are associated with colors and shapes, they can be displayed or even animated onscreen for people to recognize hidden patterns and features. Map coloring and graphical presentations of weather data are some simple examples that are familiar to everyone. This process, although it does not involve emotion and can be reproduced exactly, does output some interesting digital artwork.

In math, we often work with various quantities such as tangents, derivatives, convergence rates, and so forth. This kind of numerical information can also be visualized, and the results are often far more astonishing than you can imagine. One well-known example is fractal images. The Mandelbrot set is one of the earliest such abstract pieces of "artwork" created by the famous mathematician Benoit Mandelbrot (1924–2010), the father of fractal geometry (see Figure 1.12). Today, fractals are viewed and enjoyed by the public as digital artwork rather than their original math formulas.

Figure 1.12
The Mandelbrot set

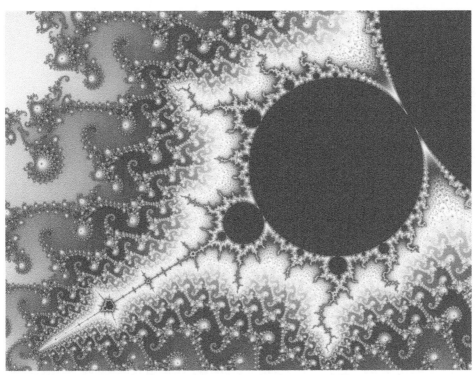

THIS IMAGE IS AVAILABLE AT http://commons.wikimedia.org/wiki/File:Mandel_zoom_08_satellite_antenna.jpg.

WHAT IS FRACTAL?

A fractal is a rough geometric shape that has a self-similarity; that is, the shape can be split into pieces, and each piece looks similar to the whole shape. In nature, trees, clouds, and mountains are perfect examples of fractals.

Using Math to Create Digital Art

The numerical representation of colors, shapes, and spaces makes math a powerful tool for generating artwork via computers. In the past several decades, the use of CG has expanded from military simulations to daily use in cartoons, movies, video games, and photo processing. With graphics software, artists are able to create an entire virtual environment and then simulate all physical properties and interactions between lights and objects.

This approach opened the door for artists to create digital artwork on the computer. In 1995, Pixar released the first computer-animated feature film, *Toy Story*, which inspired many to learn CG, and it had a huge impact in the improvement of animation production. Today, CG scientists are working day and night to invent new technologies and develop advanced algorithms for building faster and better systems. Their innovations, together with continuous improvements in computer hardware, have made graphics software the industry-standard tools for CG artists to create artwork efficiently. For instance, concept artists use Adobe Photoshop to draw and paint directly on computers, while animators create 3D models and animations via various software programs such as Autodesk Maya and 3ds Max and Pixologic's ZBrush. Motion editors manipulate video clips onscreen with Adobe After Effects.

As a result, film studios are using stunning computer-generated special effects. *Avatar*, a science-fiction film directed by James Cameron in 2009, lifted the visual-effects standard to another level with its 3D effects and its large-scale virtual world. The good news is that this revolution is just starting. Cinematic screens are becoming more like computer screens, on which moving pictures are not necessarily images of real objects but are created from "faked" digital characters and artificial props. The wonderful part of this revolution is that we are no longer restricted by any physical laws or scientific developments. Motion pictures are an arena for imagination—just like painting. You should expect more computer-generated, eye-popping digital effects in the future so that viewers can experience things that never actually happened in our universe.

While we enjoy these beautiful cinematic art products, most people don't realize how essential math is to this revolution. The technologies behind CG software are direct applications of mathematics theories. 3D objects are created with polygons and polynomial functions in an xyz-coordinate system. These concepts come from *geometry, algebra*, and *topology*—three major branches of math. Light-modeling is nothing more than math formulas that simulate the distribution of light energy. By changing the parameters of the models, we are able to replicate different materials such as stone and glass to make objects look real. Animating objects is a process of solving differential equations that describe the dynamic systems of the scene. The supporting math theories have been well studied in traditional physics.

Keep in mind, however, that, although math provides the radical and theoretical contributions for all these magical results, it is computer scientists who develop the data structures and algorithms and who implement graphics software on top of the mathematics theories. Artists are the last ones in this assembly line to finalize the imagery products.

Although software programs have brought us new media and tools for art creation, artists still may choose to mimic traditional art styles in digital space. *Non-photorealistic rendering (NPR)*, a branch of CG, is dedicated to this special type of computer art. In order to create conventional artwork numerically, researchers study the mathematics principles involved in the production process, such as pen movements and physical behaviors, media properties, or even an entire art-creation process from sketching to rendering. Although these technologies are not mature at this moment, they enable us to have fun in creating digital watercolor or oil paintings very conveniently.

Figure 1.13

A painting using IMPaSto

Figure 1.13 is an oil painting generated by an NPR system called IMPaSto developed by William Baxter et al. at the University of North Carolina at Chapel Hill in 2004. It seems that most of the traditional styles will be simulated fully by computers sooner or later, and NPR has a huge potential to create many new art styles in the future. You can visit the home page of the International Symposium on Non-Photorealistic Animation and Rendering at www.npar.org to check out the latest technical developments in this field.

Using Math in Traditional Drawing

Art is a visual communication language through which artists express their emotions. In order to do that, several art skills are required: the artist must be able to draw, master color theory, use media techniques, and be capable of artistic expression. Among these skills, drawing ability is the most essential, and it serves as the foundation of art. Just as words and grammar are critical to writing, drawing is the first skill that needs to be mastered before other techniques can be acquired.

Technically, drawing skill, sometimes referred to as *draftsmanship*, is the ability to handle lines, shapes, and gray values on 2D surfaces so that the resulting picture resembles what the artist desired or observed. In the past 200 years, especially after the invention of photography, artists were no longer constrained to realistic styles in creating their work. Nonetheless, it is still a most desirable skill to be able to draw realistically. That is why observational drawing (that is, drawing what you see) remains a core class in the curriculum of today's professional art schools.

Perspective Theory

Artists have sought out techniques to master observational drawing over thousands of years. They wanted to draw objects realistically, but an invisible magic force complicated everything: all parallel lines in the real world were no longer parallel when viewed through human vision—circles became ovals, and the size of an object varied in a strange pattern corresponding to the distance between the object and the viewer. Unable to solve these puzzles, artists couldn't efficiently create artwork that precisely resembled what they observed. They even invented devices to investigate the hidden rules governing the view (see Figure 1.14).

Figure 1.14

An ancient drawing device

THIS IMAGE IS AVAILABLE AT http://en.wikipedia.org/wiki/File:Dürer_-_Man_Drawing_a_Lute.jpg.

Without solid principles, mastering drawing was a slow process, relying solely on practice. This frustration ended in the Renaissance when art and math were integrated more closely than ever before. According to Paul Calter's book *Squaring the Circle: Geometry in Art and Architecture* (Wiley, 2008), perspective theory, the theory of how 3D objects appear on 2D surfaces, was invented by the artists Filippo Brunelleschi (1377–1446) and Leon Alberti (1404–1472). The theory was further developed by several artists including da Vinci.

It shouldn't surprise you that both Brunelleschi and da Vinci were also mathematicians, because the core foundation of perspective drawing is based on similar triangles—a simple elementary geometry problem solved a long time ago. It is interesting to note that many artists prior to the Renaissance were not able to figure out such simple geometry problems in their creative process, probably because they lacked the basic math knowledge.

Perspective theory is a big milestone in art history. "Perspective is the rein and rudder of painting," da Vinci said. The theory solves the fundamental problem of observational drawing and tells us how to draw 3D objects realistically on paper—that is, it shows us the way to draw what we actually *see*.

Sketching an object in front of us is the equivalent of projecting the object onto an imaginary 2D plane called the *picture plane*, as shown on the left side of Figure 1.15. An alternative way of understanding this process is to consider the plane as a glass window between the object and our eyes. The scene we see through the window can be viewed as an image painted on the glass—that image is what we want to draw. A side view of this scenario of mapping an object to the picture plane is shown on the right side of Figure 1.15.

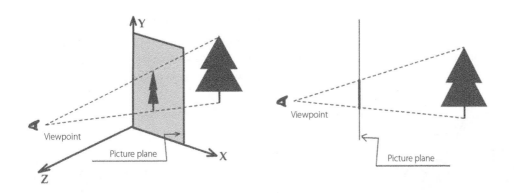

Figure 1.15
Picture plane front view (left) and side view (right)

The main idea behind perspective theory is not complicated at all. It consists of several rules based on the following key concepts:

- Horizon line or eye level
- Central vanishing point (CVP)
- Vanishing point left (VPL)
- Vanishing point right (VPR)
- Viewpoint
- Picture plane

Under a perspective projection, all straight lines in 3D space become straight lines in the picture plane. Parallel lines in a horizontal plane are no longer parallel. Instead, their extensions merge at some vanishing point on the horizon line. There are three commonly used perspective-drawing styles, depending on the number of vanishing points that are used, or equivalently, the way that an object is oriented with respect to the viewpoint. These perspective styles are as follows:

- One-point perspective
- Two-point perspective
- Three-point perspective

In-depth coverage of these styles is beyond the scope of this book. If you wish to learn further details, study the popular literature readily available.

Analytic Geometry

In 1637, French mathematician René Descartes (1596–1650) invented *analytic geometry*, also called coordinate geometry, which integrated geometry with algebra. Analytic geometry greatly increases our abilities to handle geometry problems. By using a coordinate system, spatial properties are turned into algebraic expressions so that we can use well-developed algebraic operations and theories to work through geometry challenges.

This intelligent treatment helps art too. Modern CG is probably the biggest beneficiary because its 3D modeling ability would be impossible without coordinate systems. The century-old *grid method* is a direct application of using coordinate systems for artistic purposes. Besides, analytic geometry also allows us to understand and further investigate the perspective theory with algebraic tools.

Figure 1.16

Yin and yang

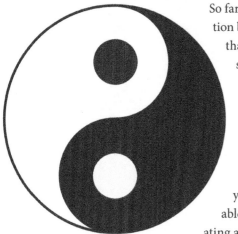

So far, I have provided you with much evidence that shows the connection between math and art. This is just a small part of the whole picture that requires much more time to discover completely. Art vs. math is similar to *yin vs. yang*, an ancient Chinese philosophical concept describing a pair of things that are polar opposites yet interconnected. Figure 1.16 illustrates the interdependencies and autonomous aspects of their coexistence.

Though perspective theory gives us a solid principle to convert 3D objects into 2D data, is it all you need to master? If not, what else should you learn? The next section presents the skills you need to acquire in order to create art. From there, you will be able to see what theories are missing and what role math plays in creating art.

Using Math to Help You Draw

Mathematics is the queen of the sciences…

—*Carl Friedrich Gauss (1777–1855), mathematician and scientist*

Math penetrates into every corner of science, engineering, and technology. By using the language of math, we can explore hidden patterns and behaviors within a real problem concerned with quantities. In turn, the results usually make us not only understand the relationship of the quantities in this particular problem better but also solve the issues with guide of the math analysis. That is why we can barely find a scientific research article that does not use math. Mathematics is a powerful tool in pushing new technologies forward in almost all fields.

In traditional drawing, the situation seems to be quite different, even though we do see the influence of math in perspective theory, which is a core aspect of today's art training. However, this theory was developed about 600 years ago, and we haven't seen any noticeable new progress since then to make the theory more efficient or easier to use. Over the past several decades, computer technology has changed almost everything in our lives by providing new solutions or improving efficiency, but traditional drawing seems to lag behind as an exception to such advances. Does that mean perspective theory is perfect and powerful enough to solve all drawing issues? If the answer is yes, then why do we still have big problems in learning how to create art efficiently? Is it because math or science is really useless in art beyond perspective theory?

This section answers these questions by presenting a new look at what we should learn in art and how math can help us. Ideally, this new analysis will give you a much clearer picture of why math should be integrated with art in order to make learning how to draw easier and faster.

Three Levels of Drawing Ability

In order to learn drawing efficiently, you first need to know what skills you have to master and what kind of approaches are practical. Therefore, this section introduces some concepts that will help you understand the drawing process and enable you to easily see the problems that can arise in learning how to draw.

We often hear the term *drawing ability* when people are talking about art training. What *is* it? What components does it contain? Is it mainly the ability of controlling your hand movements or the ability to managing graphic elements with corresponding theories? Are they acquirable? How should we obtain them? If a person uses tools to help them draw, does that person still have real drawing skill?

To make these questions even clearer, we can take an analogous look at *math ability.* How do we learn math in school? Are we taught to make our brains run faster when processing numbers, or do we learn methods so that numerical processing can be performed more intelligently and efficiently?

If a student uses a calculator to successfully complete a complicated calculation, does that dramatically improve the student's math ability? No. Obviously, students learn *methods* to gain the ability to complete math operations. This is what math instructors believe math ability is supposed to be based on. Math teachers never focus on pushing a student's neurosystem to run faster or on teaching students to do math based on *feelings* or *senses* instead of principles.

Being able to use calculators is considered an insignificant part of math abilities, although calculators are widely used in American schools. Some educators, including me, suggest that calculators should not be used by kids in elementary school because these devices cannot directly improve calculating ability. Instead, overdependence on calculators weakens a person's ability to do basic math operations such as multiplication.

Similar to math ability, there are different levels of drawing skills:

Hand-Coordination Ability This is the ability to control the movement of the dominant hand without any assistance.

Theory-Guided Drawing Ability This represents the skillfulness with which a person can draw using techniques guided by some drawing theories, but not using any extra tools such as rulers or compasses.

Tool-Assisted Drawing Ability As the name indicates, this reflects how well a person can draw when using drafting tools or devices such as rulers or even projectors.

Hand-Coordination Ability

Hand-coordination ability (HCA) represents how well your hand "listens" to your brain. It should not surprise you that HCA overlaps with the concept of eye-hand coordination in neuroscience.

A simple way to test your HCA is to draw some basic figures such as circles or straight lines directly on paper *without* any assistance. It is a well-known fact that none of us can draw them *perfectly*, although we fully understand what these graphics are supposed to resemble. This test undoubtedly tells us that everyone's HCA is limited, no matter how hard we try. This limitation can be much more noticeable when we draw large-sized figures.

You can improve HCA through practice. An obvious proof is the difference in coordination abilities between our two hands. After being trained for many years, the dominant hand of an adult can follow directions much better than the nondominant hand, even though both hands are controlled by the same brain.

Nevertheless, we can hardly push HCA beyond the bottleneck caused by physical limitations. Therefore, enhancing HCA should *not* be the major goal for art classes, because the HCA of an adult has *already* been established over many years. If improving HCA were to be a major focus, learning progress would be slow, and drawing skills would not improve significantly. We are better off teaching students to draw "smartly" instead of pushing their HCAs.

Theory-Guided Drawing Ability

Theory-guided drawing ability (TGDA) takes advantage of theories and corresponding techniques needed to draw without using any physical tools. For instance, when drawing a very large circle, we may start with a square and gradually cut its corners based on certain calculations to generate a good-looking rounded curve. Although every step in this long procedure is done without tools, the circle created can still be much better shaped than the result of drawing it freehand without a strategy—that is, using merely HCA. In this example, it is the technique that instantly increases our circle-drawing ability, although HCA is not changed at all per se. The theories used to guide our drawing may focus on various aspects, such as how to lay out structures, how to draw shapes, how to control orientations and proportions, and so forth. Using knowledge and related techniques is the key that differentiates TGDA from HCA.

Tool-Assisted Drawing Ability

Drawing with tools is like doing calculations with calculators, although drawing tools are more and more high-tech these days. If we simply judge the drawing results only, *tool-assisted drawing ability (TADA)* is appealing because it enables us to generate good artwork with little or no training. Unfortunately, TADA is not considered a real drawing skill, mainly because tools are not part of the human body. If you cannot draw without tools, you would not be called an "artist" by today's standards.

What Makes Us Draw Better?

Now that we have classified drawing ability at three levels, let's look at what we really need in order to master how to draw. Surely, TADA is not the option. Although both HCA and TGDA enable us to draw, are they equally approachable and learnable? I haven't seen any drawing books that separate these two abilities for the purpose of learning to create art, and many people consider them the same or at least inseparable. This is a major reason why incorrect drawing methods are often taught at schools.

Because the hand is the instrument doing the real work of drawing, it gives people the wrong impression that HCA and TGDA are basically the same. The truth is, these two abilities are quite different, even though related. TGDA indeed does depend on HCA, but it is drawing theory and technique that turn a person into an artist. Many artists cannot draw circles and lines much more accurately than a nonartist. Real drawing skill comes from an artist's knowledge, especially techniques that enable them to maneuver pencils on paper fluidly.

You may wonder how I know that HCA is not the driving force in an artist's drawing. In the fall of 2010, I conducted an interesting experiment that separated HCA from drawing theories and techniques. In a drawing room of the Art Institute of California, San Diego, I performed quick sketches with my *left hand*—that is, my nondominant one, for the first time in my life. You would expect my left-hand coordination ability to be terrible, because I had *never* used that hand for drawing before. Therefore, drawing with my left hand would be mainly governed by my knowledge of art and its techniques, and my poor left HCA should be of little use beyond holding a pencil and moving it slowly on paper.

However, the drawing result turned out to be a big surprise. Both the students at the scene and I were truly shocked at the quality of the 5-minute sketches I did with my left hand. One of these sketches appears on the left side of Figure 1.17. To see the influence of my right-hand HCA, a similar 5-minute quick sketch completed with my right hand appears on the right side of Figure 1.17.

In the two drawings, pronounced differences exist in the line quality and amount of work (mainly rendering) accomplished within the same time frame. Otherwise, the difference in the accuracy of structures is really unnoticeable! This test simply demonstrates that my drawing knowledge and techniques are the main force I use to manipulate lines and shapes. HCA has relatively little impact on the drawing.

When I took art classes at various educational institutions in the past, I observed that few art theories are taught besides perspective theory and human anatomy. It seems that the major goal in art classes is to improve HCA, which can be acquired with practice and a little theoretical support. Although some drawing techniques are taught, they are generally more experience-driven rather than developed systematically via principles. Such tactics sometimes go against scientific principles, although art instructors may not be aware of this.

Figure 1.17

Left-hand quick sketch (left) and right-hand quick sketch (right)

So, what are the missing pieces in today's artist training? What kind of theory can make us draw better and more efficiently? What *are* the knowledge and techniques that we should master? In my experience, drawing is a process of extracting structural information from the scene, followed by arranging geometric elements correctly on paper. Therefore, we should know how objects are structured in general and learn methods to obtain graphic elements representing the objects we want to draw. When we put pencil to paper, we must have knowledge of shapes and their spatial behaviors in 2D spaces. Additionally, we should master corresponding techniques for manipulating shapes efficiently.

The list of "must knows" is pretty short, but how well have we done so far in teaching students to master these knowledge? In the next section, you will review some of the existing methods used in today's training. I present this topic for two reasons: besides examining the usefulness of these methods in improving your drawing ability, you should know the real pros and cons of each in case you're using any of the methods discussed.

Examining Existing Drawing Methods

There are a number of popular drawing methods; some are math-driven, while some others use very little (if any) math at all. It will be helpful for you to become familiar with these methods in order to more readily learn the new method I introduce in Chapter 3, "Drawing with the ABC Method."

Perspective Drawing and Its Variations

In the previous section, I briefly mentioned the perspective theory as an application of math as well as the basic concepts involved. The theory is essential in today's art training, although some artists may not fully understand its supporting geometry theories.

To create a perspective drawing precisely, various drafting tools are typically required. Rulers, triangles, and templates are good helpers to make every line or curve perfect. Thus, executing the standard perspective drawing can be tedious and time-consuming. The method is not suitable for the outdoors, and it is often performed by professionals for commercial applications such as architecture and interior design. Figure 1.18 is a simple perspective drawing based on two vanishing points.

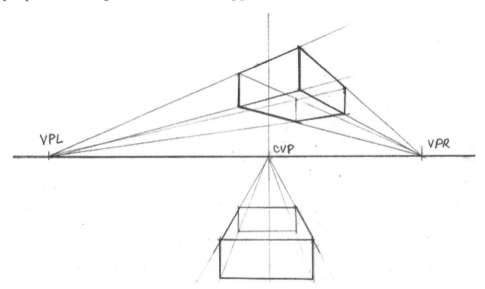

Figure 1.18

A simple perspective drawing

There are several variations of perspective drawing. The most popular one is applying perspective theory casually in order to make it more practical to use. In many situations, artists draw freehand without using tools—all points and lines are not required to be perfectly positioned and oriented. I call it *casual perspective drawing* in this book in order to differentiate it from the other versions.

In the casual perspective drawing method, perspective theory is used only as a general guide. By setting up the horizon line and vanishing points as a reference system on paper, artists can arrange shapes with respect to these references with reasonable accuracy. Most artists use this approach today.

The perspective projection is not the only way to map 3D objects onto 2D planes, however. In engineering and some video games, we often want to illustrate 3D objects without distortions. In this case, all parallel lines in a 3D space remain parallel on paper.

A simple way to do this is using *orthogonal transform*, which is theoretically equivalent to setting the viewpoint an infinite distance away from the scene in a standard perspective drawing. For this reason, we can consider this method a variation of perspective drawing. The two images in Figure 1.19 illustrate a comparison of simple cubes in perspective and orthogonal drawings. The latter is much easier for entry-level artists to draw without worrying about tedious rules.

Figure 1.19

Cubes in perspective view (left) and cubes in orthogonal view (right)

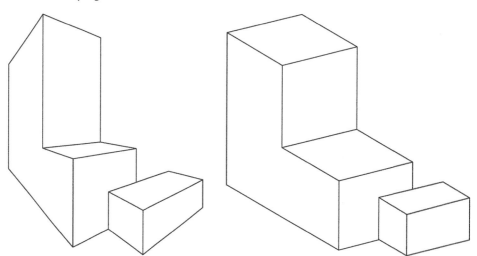

The orthogonal transform is widely used in engineering drawings for illustrating man-made objects such as car engines or pipelines. Because of the large number of components in various machines, you might think that this type of drawing would be difficult for engineers who lack art training. Amazingly, however, engineers usually don't have trouble accomplishing this complicated task. The secret is quite simple. An engineer-designed object can be deconstructed into simple, standard forms with predesigned locations and orientations. The orthogonal transform then turns 3D forms into shapes on the picture plane. All an engineer needs to do is to draw basic shapes such as ovals and rectangles in a step-by-step procedure, pretty much like solving math equations. This process is a great example that proves the power of math in drawing.

Although perspective theory is derived from math knowledge, it does not work well in all circumstances. Its application scope is limited to 3D only. If we want to copy an existing piece of 2D artwork, perspective theory is totally useless in the sense that it does not tell us how shapes in the source image should be mapped onto paper. Technically, there are no vanishing points, horizon line, or even a 3D system inside a given image upon which perspective theory arranges objects.

Using only a small number of references is another major technical weakness of perspective theory. Even in standard 3D cases, vanishing points may often occur outside the paper, and therefore this causes big operational hassles for perspective drawing. The theory handles all shapes corresponding to the few references, but is incapable of telling us the spatial relationship directly *between* shapes.

Unfortunately, managing spatial relations between shapes is the most difficult part for beginners, according to my observations. In general, it is fairly easy to draw simple shapes such as ovals or rectangles to approximate objects or components. But most of us have trouble putting these shapes at the right places with the correct orientation. Perspective theory does a very poor job in providing assistance because of its technical limitations.

The Grid Method

Whereas perspective theory fails to work for 2D images, the legendary *grid method* seems to be a good solution to fix the problem. Some art scholars consider this method an amazing way to teach people to draw 2D pictures accurately and without difficulty. By putting vertical and horizontal lines (grids) on both an original image and a paper copy, the grid system breaks the image into smaller pieces or cells that contain very simple graphics (see Figure 1.20).

This smart tactic dramatically reduces the complexity of the drawing and enables an average person to reproduce images easily. The number of grid lines depends on the size of the image to be copied, the visual complexity of the image, and the skill level of the person who is doing the drawing. The denser the grid lines, the easier the duplicating task will be. The grid system in both the original image and the paper copy must have the same number of grid lines, although the size of cells in the two systems could be different. This allows a user to enlarge or shrink the image.

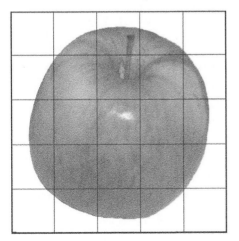
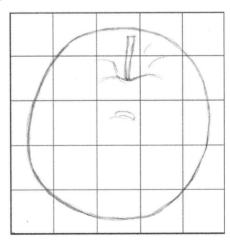

Figure 1.20

The grid method

The grid method is incredibly simple, and so is its supporting theory. A coordination system converts all spatial information into grids and uses the indices of grids to manage locations of graphical structures. This method is a direct application of analytical geometry.

Inexperienced individuals may find the grid method perfect and fall in love with it after one try. Because new users can produce highly accurate artwork, this method can boost confidence in no time. However, the grid method itself doesn't teach us any real drawing skills. Similar to tracing a picture, it does not show you how to organize graphic patterns or orient shapes except by looking at grids. In contrast, using this method excessively will degrade existing drawing skills.

Using this method for art training is similar to using calculators for learning how to do multiplication. Sadly, there are still many books on the market that promote the grid method without explaining the possible consequences it may bring. You should be aware of this crucial issue.

The grid method also suffers from a scope limitation. It is usually not feasible to set up grid lines for 3D objects. Additionally, creating grid systems isn't practical if time is critical. However, artists may use grids to reduce job complexity when they work with large-scale artwork.

I like the attractive design and powerful math principles implicitly embedded in the grid method. In fact, this was one of my major motivations to starting my math-art research—that is, to seek a new drawing approach that is as easy to use as the grid method, but tool-free and universally applicable to all objects in both 2D and 3D.

The Contour-Line Method

Many art books promote the *contour-line method,* which requires an artist to draw lines continuously while their eyes are moving along the boundaries of objects. Usually, the method is carried out *blindly*, that is, without looking at the paper during the entire drawing procedure, in order to let artist better *sense* and *feel* the objects. This unique method aims at recording the eye's movement and therefore achieves "draw what you see."

The actual results, however, are far from what might be expected. Rarely can we draw contour lines accurately—not even close. Many artists I have asked or have observed, including myself, have trouble producing good contour-line artwork in observational drawing. The image shown on the left in Figure 1.21 is an example of a contour-line sketch I did of a simple cup. Compared with my regular sketch of the same cup on the right, the contouring is terrible!

There are several scientific reasons why the contour-line method gives us poor results. When we draw, every single pencil movement produces a small error. If we continue such a task without promptly correcting the error (because our eyes are not focused on the paper), the errors will accumulate quickly to ruin the drawing.

Another piece of evidence is that an artist can hardly make a closed curve, such as the one shown on the left side of Figure 1.21, without looking at the paper. Additionally, the contour-line method mainly trains HCA without teaching any real technique to manage shapes correctly. While drawing, an artist doesn't have a chance to lay out the big picture on paper or take advantage of the graphical structures identified. Working on details without an overall plan is not a good way to solve problems in general.

The contour-line method is designed to train students to use feelings and gain a sense for drawing. In my opinion, feelings and sense are accumulated from experience. They are hardly teachable, learnable, or even describable. Students should learn solid techniques and proven knowledge from their instructors in order to master art skills efficiently.

Figure 1.21

A contour-line drawing (left) and a regular drawing (right)

The Negative-Space Method

When we draw shapes on paper, the background or blank areas are called *negative spaces*. Obviously, the negative spaces are complementary to the shapes we draw, or positive spaces. Technically, if you draw positive spaces correctly, then the negative spaces must be correct too, and vice versa. The main use of negative space is to help artists align shapes on paper. Getting an accurate spatial relationship between two shapes is accomplished by creating a correct negative space.

Figure 1.22 shows a scene with a few simple objects. The left side of the figure shows the objects, or positive spaces, in black on a white background. The right side of the figure shows the corresponding negative spaces, indicated as dark areas. Negative spaces are usually irregularly shaped, and their total number could exceed that of the corresponding positive objects. In real world, the objects have logical connections; for example, handles of clips have same thickness, and a handle is an unbroken piece even if it may be blocked by other objects. By contrast, the negative spaces are usually isolated and lack an obvious association with one another. Therefore, artists rarely use negative spaces as an independent drawing method other than an assistant tool.

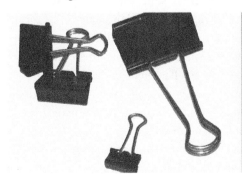 

Figure 1.22

Positive space (left) and negative space (right)

Stop Separating Math from Art

Although perspective theory is based on math theory, the art community does not emphasize the importance of math. Instead, math and art are not well-integrated, or are even separated in school curriculum. As a general rule, many artists have poor math knowledge, and technical students often cannot draw. There are surely many reasons for this problem. One of them, in my opinion, is the influence of right-brain theory.

Is the Left Brain Useless for Art?

In 1979, Betty Edwards published her famous book, *Drawing on the Right Side of the Brain* (Tarcher/Penguin). In the book, Edwards claimed that drawing is controlled mainly by the right side of the brain, and thus she suggested several unique R-mode methods to learn drawing skills.

With more than 2.5 million copies in 13 languages sold internationally, Edwards' book has certainly reshaped generations of artists over the past three decades. Many art scholars have followed her theory and ignored the importance of the left brain (or *L-mode*). Some even claimed that the left brain is useless or works counter to drawing despite the key role of perspective theory. The influence of her book on society at large is just phenomenal.

As a mathematician, artist, and computer graphics scientist, it is extremely difficult for me to accept Edwards' R-mode theory, especially the ignorance of the left brain for art, because math knowledge has helped me a lot to improve my drawing skill. First, drawing is mainly concerned with managing shapes on paper. *Applying* math knowledge to deal with geometric objects surely is a good choice, if not the best one, for that task. Perspective theory provides strong evidence of math's application to art. How is it possible that the left brain (the "logic" side) is useless for art?

Second, Edwards connected drawing with neuroscience, and thus much of her description of the R-mode is rather mysterious and hard for the average person to grasp. Teaching art by "sense" or "feeling" makes drawing less learnable. As educators, we should teach students solid theories and techniques, not mysterious "senses."

A third reason for my rejection of Edwards' hypothesis is that she suggested several R-mode methods to shut down the L-mode so that the drawing will become better *automatically* as it is handled by the right brain. This assumption is as groundless as the statement that "if you close your eyes (shut down your R-mode), your efforts to learn math will automatically be done in L-mode, and therefore you'll learn math much better." Additionally, the methods she recommended, especially the upside-down method and the contour-line method, do not provide any solid technique to help with shape management as I mentioned earlier. Both methods are aiming to improve HCA.

The most fitting part of Edwards' book is her point that beginners tend to draw from stereotyped images instead of the observed objects. This phenomenon surely is a fatal problem for beginners, and the R-mode methods can fix this problem to a certain degree. For example, the upside-down method tries to prevent an entry-level artist from recognizing any real objects. When drawing a picture, if the picture is placed upside-down, a beginner can hardly recognize the objects in the picture and thus avoid using stereotyped images. However, this treatment also stops students from taking advantage of graphic structures that exist in the scene and slows down the drawing process. Furthermore, for experienced artists who draw based on true observation, the upside-down method does not help at all but rather reduces their efficiency.

It is meaningless to debate whether the left brain is useful to art. The best way to answer this question is to deliver an efficient, logic-based drawing method, as I am doing in this book. I will provide you with a new approach that uses geometry knowledge, CG techniques, and spatial properties of objects to enable you to draw efficiently. You will see how drawing can be improved by some simple math applications. Ideally, this non-conventional method will correct the ill-informed attitude toward math that exists in the art community. Art and math should be merged together just as they were in the time of the Renaissance.

Learning Art with the Full Brain

As pointed out in Edwards' book, logic and reasoning are functions of the left brain, and visual activity is a function of the right brain. In my opinion, the different functionalities of the two hemispheres of the brain perfectly match two of the levels of drawing abilities I defined earlier. HCA is related to spatial sense and thus belongs to the right brain, while TGDA applies to the logical and analytical thinking done in the left brain. Drawing is a process that uses both abilities, although TGDA is much more teachable and learnable than HCA.

Currently, we still don't have enough scientific methods to help us fully control our drawing. Perspective theory is far from a perfect solution. It is time to develop more solid scientific methods so that everyone can easily learn to draw. This book is an attempt to guide you in mastering draftsmanship skills scientifically and efficiently.

Over the past few years, I have hosted numerous workshops on my math-oriented drawing method for different audiences, including art faculties and students at the Art Institute of California, San Diego, and for computer science students at Zhejiang University, China. The result has been very promising. Some tech-minded audiences saw a quick surge in their drawing ability after just a few days!

I think the art community needs to move forward to bring math into art in order to better understand and control spatial properties. The math logic in the left brain definitely helps our art that is naturally connected with the visual acuity of the right brain. Learning art should be a full-brain experience!

CHAPTER 2

Extracting Graphical Structures— A Scientific Point of View

Learning to draw is learning to see. —Anonymous

In Chapter 1, "Understanding the Relationship between Math and Art," you were told that the drawing process comprises two major components: extracting shapes from a scene and managing those shapes on paper. It is now time to address the first part. Clearly, this task does not have a unique approach, because different artists may obtain different information from the same scene, especially if emotion is involved. However, this chapter presents a standard method for processing graphic information— much like anatomy theory does for figure drawing. By observing objects scientifically, drawing becomes much easier and more efficient.

Over the past several decades, computer graphics (CG) scientists have developed many useful concepts and techniques that are used in today's cartoons, movies, and video games. These techniques are designed to make processing and storing graphic data accurate and fast. Some of these CG principles are applicable to traditional drawing as well. So why don't we take advantage of these existing approaches?

This chapter uses CG techniques to address the following issues:

- How objects are structured

- Spatial properties of shapes

- What graphical structures should be extracted for drawing purposes

- How triangulation is used to extract graphic information

Introducing CG Concepts and Principles

In CG, a 3D scene may contain hundreds or even thousands of objects. In order to create realistic images for such complicated scenes, CG scientists have worked several decades to develop concepts, algorithms, and principles to make generating images fast and accurate.

Creating digital images with computers is similar to traditional observational drawing. Both processes aim to generate realistic images of a scene from a given viewpoint. Although the human brain has neither the same computing ability nor the massive memory of a powerful computer, the basic technologies used in CG can still be of great help to traditional drawing. This section introduces you to several CG principles for managing massive-scale pictorial information.

Divide and Conquer

One principle used for problem solving in modern computer science is *divide and conquer*. This principle says that we can split a large-scale problem into smaller subproblems of the same type. After we find solutions to all the subproblems, we can then combine them to solve the original problem.

In CG applications such as video games, interactive rendering for 3D scenes frequently requires computing power that is beyond the capabilities of standard PCs. The divide-and-conquer principle greatly reduces computation complexity by processing a small portion of the scene separately.

Divide and conquer is a general strategy applicable to areas outside computer science. The grid method mentioned in Chapter 1 is considered an application of this principle. In the grid method, a large image is chopped into small cells, and the artist duplicates the image cell by cell instead of working on the entire image at once.

It should be pointed out, however, that the divide-and-conquer approach involves more than just dividing a big piece into smaller ones. The integration of subproblem solutions is essential to solving the original problem. Typically, integration requires a systematic solution and special techniques to glue all the small pieces together. For example, in drawing a large and complex scene, you can draw small parts according to the divide-and-conquer principle. However, drawing each component accurately does not guarantee the correctness of the whole picture. You must arrange these pieces carefully to get a correct solution for the whole scene.

Multiresolution and Hierarchical Approaches

An extremely useful way to solve large-scale problems efficiently is to take a *multiresolution* or hierarchical approach. In CG, *resolution* means the degree of detail or complexity. If we want to solve a complicated problem but have a time restriction, trying to solve the whole problem at once is not a good idea, because that may take longer than the time allows. For example, creating a crystal-clear digital image from a large, complicated 3D scene may take seconds or even minutes on an average PC. This speed surely does not meet the requirements of interactive CG applications such as flight simulations or 3D first-person shooting games. Typically, several actions are taken to reduce the computation cost, including using texture mappings and a set of models at different levels of detail (LOD). However, a multiresolution approach provides a general-purpose problem-solving principle by trading off image quality and processing time. With this strategy, many graphics software programs will generate a low-quality (coarse-resolution) image first and then keep refining it until time runs out.

In observational drawing, we usually don't have a firm time restriction. However, when an artist creates quick sketches in a public place, the time allowed is much shorter—perhaps counted in seconds. In this case, a multiresolution approach is surely a smart choice. Figure 2.1 shows a detailed curve drawn at different resolutions, from low to high.

Figure 2.1

Curve drawn at different resolutions

Progressive/Adaptive Refinement

Progressive/adaptive refinement is a general strategy naturally associated with multiresolution approaches. Typically, we express a target problem in a hierarchical structure so that we can access the lowest level first and gradually add details to achieve higher quality.

Progressive refinement is highly desirable on the Web, where users want to view large images instantly. Instead of requiring the user to wait a long time to view a high-quality image, a computer can display a lower-quality image first and then refine it continuously as the user is browsing. This is also done via *progressive JPGs* when processing large images.

Remember the contour-line method discussed in Chapter 1? It is quite clear that contouring is not a multiresolution approach. Directly drawing details (that is, drawing the finest level) does not give us any flexibility in balancing quality and speed. Therefore, contouring cannot take advantage of constructing graphic details progressively, layer by layer.

Boolean Operations

Boolean operations represent mathematical logic processes that integrate two sets or objects. By using these operations—called *union*, *intersection*, and *difference*—different results can be generated from the two given objects. Figure 2.2 shows two objects, a square (A) and a circle (B), and the outcomes of Boolean operations on them.

Figure 2.2

Boolean operations

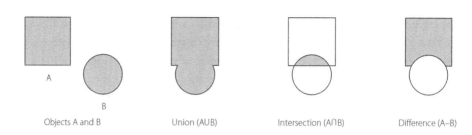

Objects A and B   Union (A∪B)   Intersection (A∩B)   Difference (A–B)

Boolean operations offer us a powerful mechanism to deconstruct a complicated object into simpler and smaller ones. Obviously, we can apply these operations repeatedly on the subobjects to divide everything further into trivial items. This treatment is a direct application of the divide-and-conquer strategy in dealing with geometric objects.

Primary Forms and CSG Trees

In a 3D physical space, objects may have various appearances. Some are smooth, some are rough, some are complicated, and some are simple. In order to study their behaviors, mathematicians have simplified and categorized objects into several primary forms: spheres, cubes, cylinders, cones, and torus (see Figure 2.3).

Figure 2.3

Primary object forms

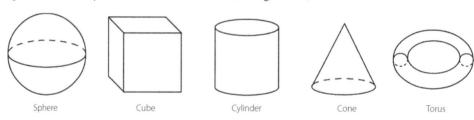

Sphere   Cube   Cylinder   Cone   Torus

Although the primary forms represent just a few 3D structures, their combination with Boolean operations and *transforms* (positions, rotations, and scales) enable us to create almost any object.

A *constructive solid geometry (CSG)* tree is a graphic representation that is used by computer-aided design (CAD) software to build 3D objects with the primary forms. Figure 2.4 shows a simple CSG process that produces a fairly complicated object with a few Boolean operations. Because the process manipulates an object based on other objects, it can be illustrated as a tree structure—a popular diagram used in computer science.

A CSG tree is a mathematical tool used to analyze the internal structure of an object. More important, its process is designed so that it can be used directly to assemble objects with Boolean operations step-by-step. In recent decades, mathematicians have used this principle to produce *fractals*, which, as you saw in Chapter 1, are special objects with infinite levels of detail and self-similarities. A graphic is said to have self-similarity if its components appear similar to the whole structure.

Figure 2.5 is a 3D fractal that repeatedly adheres smaller spheres to any existing sphere. Figure 2.6 is the famous Koch curve. It starts by chopping a line segment (indicated as *level 1*) into three equal-length pieces, and then it replaces the middle one with two equal-sized segments to form an equilateral configuration. The result is referred to as *level 2*. This simple constructive rule is then applied recursively to each line segment in the figure. Finally, the line converts into a detailed curve, as shown in the bottom of the figure.

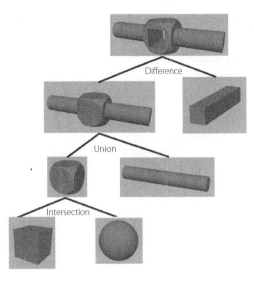

Figure 2.4
CSG tree

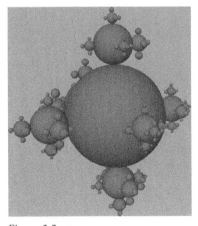

Figure 2.5
A 3D fractal

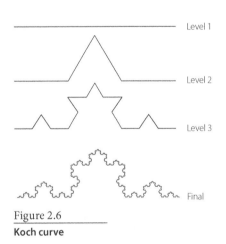

Figure 2.6
Koch curve

In nature, clouds, trees, and terrain are all composed of fractal structures because of their self-similarities. Many video games use fractals to generate realistic plants and terrains. Doing so is simple and efficient.

Bounding Boxes and Polygons

Although most CG techniques are developed to produce complicated objects, sometimes it is necessary to do the opposite. A bounding box can be used to accomplish this goal.

A *bounding box* is the tightest box that can surround an object, no matter how complicated that object is. Thus, a bounding box can be viewed as a simplified version of the original object. The major purpose of such treatment is to describe the size, proportion, and location of an object without processing its detailed information.

The left image in Figure 2.7 shows the bounding box of a 2D image of an airplane. Obviously, a box (either a 3D cube or 2D rectangle) is not able to approximate an object very well. However, because of their simplicity, bounding boxes are widely used in CG for quick geometry processing.

Figure 2.7

Bounding box (left) and bounding polygon (right)

A bounding box cannot be used to draw an object because it is a rather poor approximation. However, a *bounding polygon* is a related concept that can be used for drawing purposes. A bounding polygon is similar to a bounding box, except we replace the box with a convex polygon.

> **CONVEX AND CONCAVE POLYGONS**
>
> In math, a polygon is *convex* if none of its internal angles is more than 180°; otherwise, it is known as *concave*.

The right image in Figure 2.7 shows a bounding polygon for the same airplane. Bounding polygons can approximate the silhouette of an object very closely. Therefore, polygons are helpful in drawing.

Triangulation and Triangle Meshes

Triangulation is an important technique used in CG for managing spatial information. For a given set of points in an image, we can connect them to form a *triangle mesh* that covers the entire image. The main purpose of triangulation is to partition a 2D region into triangles so that all structures under the triangle mesh can be quickly located and studied.

The left image in Figure 2.8 shows a simple triangulation built on a few points selected from a picture of cans. Clearly, sometimes we want to triangulate an area of interest only. I call this *local triangulation*. The right image in Figure 2.8 shows an example of local triangulation compared with the global triangulation example in the image shown on the left.

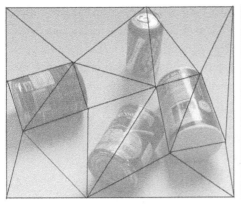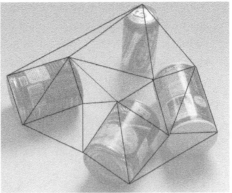

Figure 2.8

Global triangulation (left) and local triangulation (right)

DELAUNAY TRIANGULATION

For a given set of points, there are many ways to connect them for a triangulation. In other words, there is no one "right" way. However, some triangles, such as long, thin ones, are not as symmetrically shaped as equilateral triangles and therefore are avoided in some types of triangulation. *Delaunay triangulation*, for instance, maximizes the angles within the triangles. This type of triangle quality is important for engineering calculations, because a very skinny triangle can cause instability of computations in computers. But it is not a big issue in this book as I use triangulation for extracting and managing shapes. There is no computation involved, and we will never intentionally create very skinny triangles in drawing.

Triangulation is very much like the traditional grid method in the sense that both techniques partition a region into smaller regions. However, there are several critical differences:

- A triangle is a stable structure, whereas a rectangle is not. (Imagine a triangle and a square made of flexible straws. If you were to pull or push on a side of each shape, the triangle would not deform, because each side braces the two other sides, but the square would.) This math property simply means that a triangle mesh cannot be stretched, but a grid system is stretchable. In other words, if we use both systems to describe spatial information, triangulation is more reliable and error-proof.

- The second difference is in flexibility. A triangulation can be implemented for any number of points at any location, whereas grid lines must be uniformly spaced. This aspect translates to a higher efficiency of triangulation over grids.

- Triangles can approximate curves much faster than rectangles. In CG, the so-called 'quadtree technique' uses a combination of rectangles to represent a 2D shape. The left image in Figure 2.9 shows how a quadtree approximates a quarter of a circle, while the right image in Figure 2.9 is a triangulated version of that same quarter of a circle. No doubt that the triangulation is much more efficient in fewer steps.

Despite these benefits of triangulation, it is harder to create and manage than grids.

Figure 2.9

The quadtree approach (left) and the triangulation approach (right)

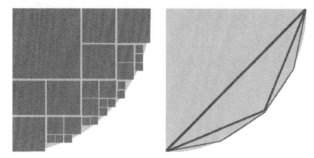

Because triangulation works for any number of points, it automatically has the capability for adaptive refinement. In other words, we can always insert new points into an existing triangle mesh by re-triangulating it with the updated vertices set. If a small number of points are added, then the re-triangulation needs to be done only at the places where new vertices are added. This feature allows us to perform a triangulation in a hierarchical manner or a multiresolution style by adding vertices progressively.

Figure 2.10 shows a three-level triangulation of Abraham Lincoln's image on Mount Rushmore. During the triangulation, the user can keep adding facial landmarks for triangulation that divide the image into smaller regions as desired. Such treatment is useful for effectively controlling graphical structures in an image, as you will see in Chapter 3.

Figure 2.10

Progressive refinement of a triangulation

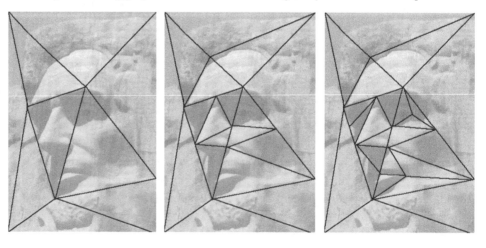

SOME ISSUES IN TRIANGULATION

In CG, a triangulation does not allow any vertex of a triangle to sit in the middle of another triangle. Otherwise, it will generate a *T-bone* structure, as shown in the left image of Figure 2.11. A T-bone is bad in CG because it creates a crack in 3D triangle meshes. But it is not harmful for drawing purposes in this book as we use only for 2D images.

Technically, a T-bone can be easily fixed by adding an additional line, as shown in the right image of Figure 2.11. However, this process increases complexity of the triangulation without benefit to us and thus will not be used here. You'll find many T-bones in Figure 2.10.

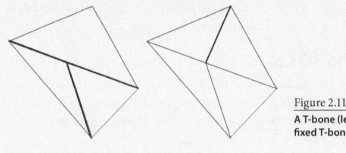

Figure 2.11
A T-bone (left) and a fixed T-bone (right)

When a new point is inserted into an existing triangulation (see the left image of Figure 2.12), there are two kinds of re-triangulation approaches. A simple way is to identify which existing triangle contains the point and then partition that triangle with the newly inserted point (see the center image of Figure 2.12). Although this easy method does not affect any other triangles in the mesh, it will quickly generate very thin triangles if more points are added in the same area (see the right image of Figure 2.12). Therefore, this approach is not suggested in CG.

Figure 2.12
Re-triangulation with a single triangle partitioning

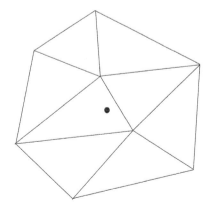
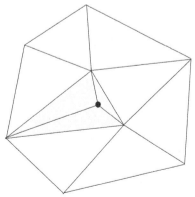
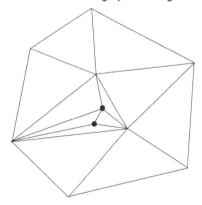

Figure 2.13

Re-triangulation with a regional repartitioning

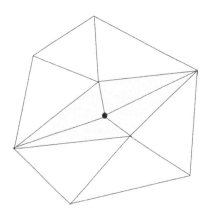

A second method is to re-triangulate the region near the place where a new point is inserted. Figure 2.13 shows a regional re-triangulation in the shaded area for the same point indicated earlier. This approach generates better-looking triangles but affects more areas in the existing triangle mesh.

In this book, both of the re-triangulation schemes are acceptable. However, a rule of thumb is to use the edges of triangles to represent important patterns in an image.

Unifying 2D and 3D Cases

In the previous chapter, you learned that perspective theory does not work for 2D images because there is no depth to compress. You cannot use vanishing points if you wish to duplicate a nonrealistic drawing or a texture design. This is a serious limitation for the theory when we consider it for a generic drawing solution.

In observational drawing, an ideal method should help us draw *whatever* we see. Whether the target object is 2D or 3D, a landscape or a human figure, we want to use a drawing method that works well in all circumstances without changing its basic principles. The difference between drawing a real teacup and a portrait photo, for instance, should be based on how much *extra* help we can get from each object's particular graphical structure. For example, in drawing the human face, the anatomical configuration allows us to use eye-line, nose-line, and mouth-line for a better arrangement of facial features. When we draw a teacup, the extra help comes from its cylindrical form. In both cases, the fundamental approach to laying out graphics on paper should remain the same. In this section, you will learn a new approach for unifying all 2D and 3D cases.

Images on the Picture Plane

To find a universal method suitable for any scene, we must first answer this fundamental question: What is the common and essential element of *all* scenes? A simple answer is *the images on the picture plane.*

Recall that the picture plane in perspective theory is an imaginary plane in front of our eyes. It acts as a window through which we see the world. Theoretically, there are two picture planes for a human vision system—each eye has one. These two planes are slightly different, and they enable us to sense the depth of an object in 3D space. If you close one eye, you will see no difference between a 2D picture and a 3D object projected on the picture plane.

Artists usually call the process of closing one eye *flattening objects,* which will help artists better draw 3D objects on paper. In other words, any object we see can be considered an image on the picture plane, whether the object is 2D or 3D. This feature allows us to unify all scenes as images on the picture plane. If we find an efficient method to draw these images, we then are able to handle all types of scenes. Therefore, throughout the rest of this book, the main focus is to explore how to draw 2D images, although the original scene could be 3D.

The Role of Perspective Theory

Dealing with flattened images can greatly simplify our drawing process. In math, structures and spatial relationships in 3D are far more complicated than in 2D images in general. Although this strategy sounds good, we now hit a dead end in perspective theory. Does that mean we are going to ignore or abandon the theory? How can we still use the well-established theory to draw 2D images in the picture plane? What role will perspective theory play?

Technically speaking, perspective theory provides simple rules about how 3D *parallel lines* and circles are positioned in 2D space, corresponding to a few reference lines and vanishing points. It works best for objects with many parallel edges, such as cubes or buildings. A circle becomes an oval in the perspective view and thus is not too hard to use. For an arbitrarily shaped object, we can find its projection on paper by looking at its bounding box under the perspective theory. But this process could be very complicated if a 3D structure contains many irregular forms, such as flowers and plants. Moreover, the theory does not show us directly how multiple objects are related to each other on paper. Moving into the picture plane is an attempt to solve these 2D shape problems in 2D space directly, rather than within a 3D space. However, perspective theory is still useful for handling a *single* object, especially regularly formed mechanical parts or objects with a simple form. This is exactly how many art teachers use the theory in observational drawing instruction.

Figure 2.14 is a popular type of drawing seen in art schools today. In this drawing, each object is well described by ovals and deformed parallel lines by using perspective theory. However, the theory is almost useless in guiding us on laying out the overall configuration.

The major role of perspective theory is to help us understand and draw simple forms more *accurately.* This role is particularly important in designing when artists sketch using their imagination. In observational drawing, however, our vision system already projects all 3D objects onto the picture plane by using the *same* perspective transform. Theoretically, it is not necessary to apply perspective theory anymore. Still, today's artists typically apply the theory by using the following long and detoured process:

1. A 3D object is projected as a 2D image on the picture plane by our eyes with a perfect perspective transform.

Figure 2.14

A 3D perspective drawing

2. Based on the image observed, an artist figures out its original 3D form.

3. The artist then applies the theory to the 3D form and obtains its shape information in order to draw the *image* he or she sees on paper.

Why can't we just draw the projected image directly? If we are able to draw all images on the picture plane we *see*—that is, arranging each object on paper with the correct location, proportion, orientation, and spatial relationship to other objects, then the result is a perfect perspective drawing. Studying and managing 2D images is exactly what you will learn in this book. It is more effective and applicable to all subject areas to draw from images on the picture plane directly rather than drawing real objects from 3D space.

Basic Shapes

When drawing objects, you should not draw their silhouettes directly as in the contour-line method. Instead, it is better to sketch out the overall structure before adding details.

Such a hierarchical approach not only simplifies the drawing process but flattens your learning curve as well.

In order to draw big pictures of objects, artists traditionally use a variety of *basic shapes*, typically ovals, rectangles or squares, and triangles. These 2D shapes are the foundations for all other, more-complex configurations.

In the previous section, you were introduced to the primary (3D) forms that are used to construct 3D objects. Once projected onto 2D paper, these 3D forms are turned into a union of polygons and ovals. Figure 2.15 shows examples of cubes and cones. Although a polygon is made from triangles, polygons and ovals are selected as the basic shapes featured in this book for working with triangulation strategy. In the next chapter, you will see how polygons can be used as a way to efficiently manipulate shapes. Another reason to design a new basic shape set is that rectangles and triangles are all unified under the concept of polygons. This tactic will simplify learning to draw basic shapes.

Figure 2.15

Some 3D primary forms (left) and their projections in 2D space (right)

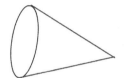
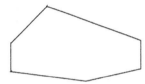
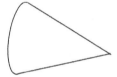

These basic shapes serve as the building blocks of observational drawing. For beginners, it is essential to learn how to handle these simple shapes efficiently on paper. This is akin to the "addition" operation when learning math. You have to master it before moving to an upper level. The good news is that most people don't have any trouble copying these shapes. After an entry-level artist has acquired the skill to draw basic shapes, drawing theories and techniques will help that artist conquer all types of complicated shapes and combinations. That is why art is not only a subject that can be learned but one that is easy to learn as well.

Understanding the Properties of Basic Shapes

Basic shapes will be your tools for drawing everything you see. To learn how to draw efficiently, you must understand and familiarize yourself with the geometric properties of these structures.

Ovals

In artwork, an *oval* usually comes from a sphere or circle in 3D space. An oval has many useful geometric properties, including two axes: a *major axis* (*long axis*) and a *minor axis* (*short axis*), as shown in Figure 2.16. The two axes are perpendicular to each other—that is, they form a 90-degree angle. Their intersection is the *center* of the oval. The longest distance from the center to the side of the oval is the major radius, which occurs along the long axis to either side of the oval. Similarly, the *minor radius* is present on the short axis.

An oval is symmetric with respect to both the major and minor axes. This property is useful in helping us make hand-drawn ovals symmetric. In Figure 2.16, an oval is inscribed inside a rectangle (or bounding box). The length of the box is twice that of the major radius, and its width is twice that of the minor radius.

Figure 2.16

An oval structure

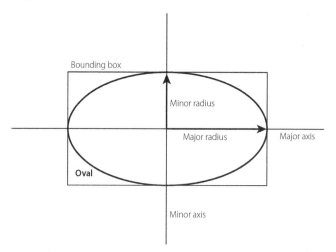

Visually, the configuration of the bounding rectangle (its length vs. its width) determines the proportion of the oval, or the thickness/thinness of its appearance. The most efficient way to determine the size of an oval is create its bounding box. After you build the surrounding rectangle, the oval is easily established.

The bounding box of a circle is a square. Therefore, a circle is treated as a special case of an oval without a separate discussion in this book.

Polygons

A *polygon* is a 2D, closed figure that contains at least three sides. None of its sides should intersect with any of its other sides. Many types of polygons are seen in our daily lives: triangles, squares/rectangles, pentagons, and hexagons. In math, we usually use the term n-gon to refer a polygon that has n sides, where n is any whole number equal to or greater than three.

A polygon does not necessarily have equal-sized sides, and a polygon can be convex or concave. This flexibility makes a polygon the perfect tool to approximate arbitrary graphic shapes. Many artists love to use polygons to draw smooth objects. Not only does it simplify curves, but it also makes soft objects look very appealing and strong.

A polygon can be disassembled into triangles, and the way to accomplish this is not unique. Figure 2.17 shows two ways to partition the same 6-gon, or hexagon. This property will be extremely useful in our new drawing method, because it indicates that we can always control a complicated polygon shape easily via simple triangles. This strategy can be viewed as divide and conquer as well.

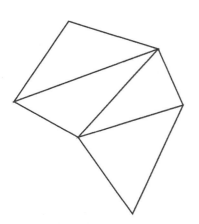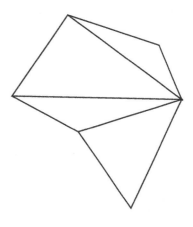

Figure 2.17

**Partitioning
a polygon in
different ways**

Another way to represent a polygon is to use a multiresolution approximation. For a
large *n*-gon, we may create a triangle (3-gon) or quadrilateral (4-gon) as a coarse model.
By increasing the number of points, we can approach the final version via a sequence of
polygons at different resolutions, or levels of detail. Figure 2.18 shows one such sequence
used to build a complicated polygon.

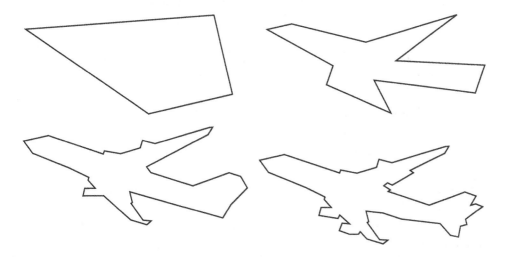

Figure 2.18

**Coarse polygon (top
left), after adding
more points (top
right), adding more
points still (bottom
left), and the final
polygon (bottom
right)**

Degrees of Freedom

A key issue in drawing is managing a shape's transforms—in other words, its location,
rotation, and proportion (scaling). When we have a shape, say, a rectangle, there are many
ways to manipulate it, including stretching it vertically and/or horizontally or rotating it.
This fact simply tells us that we have to solve for several uncertainties in order to make a
shape what we want.

Figure 2.19 shows a simple, square graphic and two variations after different scaling and/or rotation operations are applied. In math, we call these uncertainties *variables*. But there is a better term from mechanics, called *degrees of freedom* (DOF). Mechanical engineers use DOF to refer to the set of operations needed to orient a component correctly in a system.

Figure 2.19
A graphic and its variations

It is easy to see from Figure 2.19 that a *single* object has a DOF of three. In other words, if we want to duplicate a single shape on paper, we need to determine three variables: vertical scaling, horizontal scaling, and rotation. After we take care of these three issues, the shape will be completely fixed. For a single shape, it does not matter where you put it on paper. Therefore, location is not part of the DOF for drawing an individual object.

However, when we consider a scene or a group of objects, every individual object has five DOFs because its position, or displacement in both horizontal and vertical directions, really counts. For example, to draw a human face correctly, we have to arrange each of its features, say, the nose, in the correct proportion, rotation, and position. The position of each component affects the spatial relationship with the rest of the scene. Technically, if a scene includes 10 rectangles, in order to draw this simple system correctly, we need to fix 50 uncertainties in total!

Generally speaking, we have many more individual objects and components to draw in observational drawing. This explains why drawing is hard—it is a large system consisting of a huge number of DOFs. Even if people can draw individual items such as a nose or eye correctly, it does not mean they can draw a good face! The most difficult part of drawing is not how to draw basic shapes but rather how to solve the DOFs.

The DOF analysis explains why the drawing methods described in Chapter 1 do a poor job, because none of them provides a systematic solution for how to solve all the DOFs in a drawing. A good drawing method must have a solid solution to determine positions, rotations, and proportions of objects.

Understanding Graphical Structures

Now that you have reviewed the properties of shapes, you are ready to tackle the main purpose of this chapter: understanding the graphical structures you need to extract from a scene and how to acquire them. The term *graphical structure (GS)* refers to any lines or shapes in an image.

SEEING THE FOREST FROM THE TREES

A beginner who sits in front of a scene and attempts to draw it will quite often become overwhelmed by the degree of detail embedded in the objects. I still remember a frustrating moment when I was in middle school in China. One day, I went to a mountain to draw forests with a group of kids. Not one among us had any observational drawing training. Looking at a countless number of trees, bushes, and rocks, I was completely overwhelmed and had no clue where to get started. What I was seeing everywhere were details instead of the big picture. Not understanding how to obtain useful graphical structures is common for untrained would-be artists.

There are all kinds of graphic patterns in a scene, such as ovals, rectangles, triangles, spheres, cones, cylinders, symmetry, repetition, linear alignments, and so on. Which of these graphic patterns do we need to notice in order to draw a scene? The answer is directly related to what we *can* draw. Usually, we draw only simple *shapes* and *lines* at a reasonable level of detail. We are not able to draw complicated objects like a whole tree or an entire human body quite accurately at a single step. So, first we must determine the graphical structures we need in order to draw these shapes and lines. We rarely sketch micro-level features or textures unless it is absolutely necessary. Additionally, a graphical structure has no minimum size. A small GS always contains various smaller features. This characteristic suggests that we must start with the big picture and gradually add the details. An opposite approach, such as the contour-line method of drawing, can easily overwhelm a learner with a large number of mini-graphic features.

Static vs. Dynamic Graphical Structures

Every object has its own structure. A bottle has a body, a neck, and a head. A chair has a seat, a back, and several legs. These elements are *static graphical structures*, because they never change during the drawing process. People may or may not know much about these elements despite their obvious existence.

Artists have studied human anatomy, the static structures of our bodies, over many hundreds of years. When it comes to the human face, many books will tell you the spatial relationship between eyes, nose, mouth, ears, and so on. Figure 2.20 shows how facial structures are analyzed with measurements so that artists can duplicate or design a head with ease. Today, the study of human anatomy is essential training for all professional art students.

Figure 2.20

Static GSs in a human face

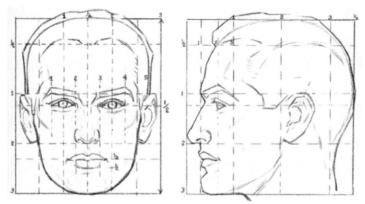

Unfortunately, artists rarely study the static GSs for objects other than human and animal bodies. Part of the reason is that most objects don't have a standard anatomical system. Nevertheless, we must admit that using a static GS is helpful. It is like a blueprint in engineering. Without such assistance, there is no way to create complicated objects such as automobiles or airplanes.

Although static GSs are important in helping us to understand the object in order to draw it better, dynamic GSs are the ones we really need to obtain. *Dynamic graphical structures* are those that form based on the particular environment at a particular moment in time. Many factors dynamically affect such patterns: orientation of an object, movements of mobile components, viewer's position and angle, lighting and shadowing, blockage of other objects, and so forth. For instance, when we look at athletes on a field or dancers performing on stage, the mobility of the human body creates a huge number of dynamic GSs. Figure 2.21 shows a simple, quick sketch of a dancer in which several dynamic polygons can be easily spotted.

Based on my observation, quite a few beginning art students stick with the static GSs after taking an anatomy class. When advancing to a quick-sketch class, they often feel frustrated because some static structures are distorted or not even visible because of the viewing angle. The correct approach should be to extract and sketch those dynamic structures while keeping the static ones as references.

Figure 2.21

**Dynamic graphi-
cal structures in a
human body**

Individual vs. Grouped graphical Structures

Another way to look at graphical structures is as individual vs. grouped. An *individual
graphical structure* (or *internal graphical structure*) is inside an individual object, whereas
a *grouped graphical structure* (or *external graphical structure*) is formed jointly with multiple objects. The former is pretty easy to understand, because an individual item always
has its own structures. The latter represents those patterns involving different items. A
simple example is that when a person sits on a chair, that person's body parts will combine with the chair or other surrounding objects to create various interesting GSs. Such
structures express the connections between different objects and thus are important for
orienting objects on paper.

Figure 2.22 demonstrates several individual and grouped graphical structures in a
simple scene. Two individual GSs are drawn with thick lines (representing the statue's
legs and the statue's torso and arms), and a group GS (triangle) is highlighted (representing the statue and the bench).

Figure 2.22

Individual vs. grouped GSs

Traditionally, artists use negative space as a tool for aligning objects. Usually, negative space contains many small, irregularly shaped pieces that are not very efficient or applicable for managing big pictures. Grouped GSs can be used to overcome the drawback of negative space. By merging concerning items together to form a new regular shape, the resulting GS will contain (part of) negative space between the items. Therefore, we can control the negative space via the GS. Figure 2.23 shows how the negative space is naturally taken into consideration in the three grouped GSs (highlighted). If we can duplicate these simple shaped GSs, the clips in the image will be arranged correctly.

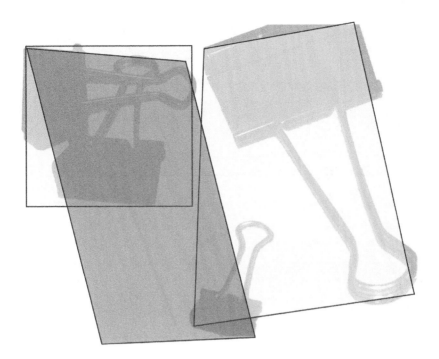

Figure 2.23

Grouped GSs can be used to control negative space

Multiresolution Graphical Structures

One way to achieve high efficiency is to use hierarchical or multiresolution approaches. In drawing, this means outlining objects from a big framework down to detailed features or from coarse levels down to fine levels. This is easier said than done, because the target scene itself generally does not provide such an image hierarchy. It is incumbent upon the artist to identify and organize the information in a multiresolution way before starting to draw on paper.

There are various ways to create a multiresolution expression for a scene. A simple one is to start with the area of interest and approximate it with a simple polygon. Whether it is an individual GS or a grouped GS, this polygon serves as the base, or the coarsest level, of the graphics hierarchy. The next step is to obtain finer-level structures by identifying smaller polygons inside this polygon. This process can be repeated until all GSs are small enough to handle without issue.

Figure 2.24 illustrates one example of creating such a multiresolution approximation. In this instance, only four levels are displayed. We can see that graphical structures at each level are very dynamic, as the human body is very transformable. This process can continue for a couple of more steps in the face area, as eyes, nose, and mouth must be further separated from each other. The dotted line on the face is the so-called center line in art books. It is a kind of static structure, but beginners can hardly figure out such structures without instructions or reading anatomy books.

Figure 2.24

Base polygon (top
left), second level
(top right), third
level (bottom left),
and fourth level
(bottom right)

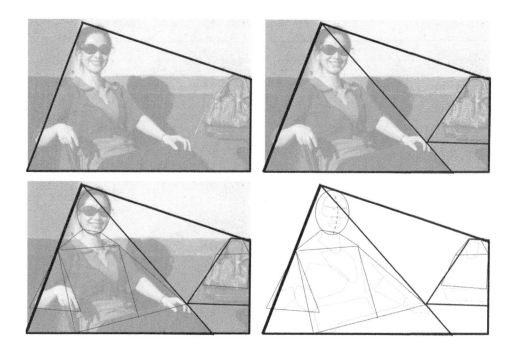

A multiresolution representation for a given scene is not unique because most GSs
are dynamic and grouped. Each artist will select these GSs differently and arrange them
based on personal interests and preferences. The selection does not matter, as long as the
artist uses a solid hierarchical approach and follows that hierarchy to lay out the various
GSs identified.

You may have observed that more polygons are used than ovals in the preceding
example. Although we can use ovals to approximate any structures at any level, ovals
often suffer the following drawbacks:

- Most graphical structures are not close to oval shapes.
- Unlike polygons, we cannot divide an oval into smaller ovals perfectly.
- An oval does not have corner points on its boundary, and thus it is hard for us to use
  any fixed point on the oval as a visual reference.

The only time we really need to use ovals is when a graphic is really an oval-like shape,
such as a plate, a cup, or a human face.

However, technically, multiresolution is a strategy that is not limited to polygons. As
a comparison, two more hierarchical approaches are presented here, using ovals and
rectangles, respectively. In both Figure 2.25 and Figure 2.26, thick lines represent earlier
coarse resolutions. The thickness is reduced as the details are refined.

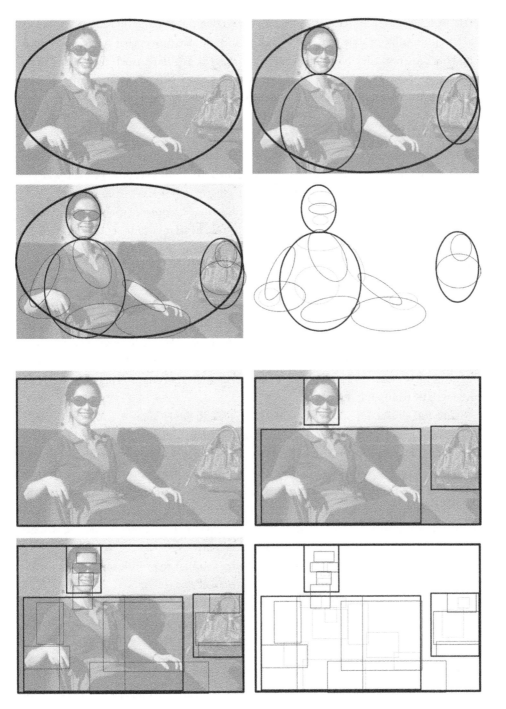

Figure 2.25
Base oval (top left), second level (top right), third level (bottom left), and fourth level (bottom right)

Figure 2.26
Base rectangle (top left), second level (top right), third level (bottom left), and fourth level (bottom right)

Figure 2.26 uses rectangles only, which implies that the grid method can be modified into a multiresolution style too. However, the example also proves that vertical and horizontal lines are not a flexible and efficient approach to irregular shapes, despite the simplicity of using rectangles. This is a major reason why polygons and triangulation meshes are used instead of rectangles in this book to solve drawing problems.

Extracting GSs with Triangulation

Earlier in this chapter, you learned about triangulation, a technique widely used in computer graphics to describe and store spatial information. In this section, you will learn how to obtain triangulation or corresponding triangulation meshes from images.

The fundamental principle of observational drawing is acquiring graphical structures that are easy to draw. Triangle meshes, or a collection of triangles, are good tools to help us achieve this goal. They are flexible enough to approximate any shapes. They are multiresolution in the sense that we can refine a mesh by adding more points followed by a re-triangulation.

Although these features are helpful, an extremely useful and important feature of triangle meshes is their stability for building a framework in a 2D plane. A triangle mesh is like a web. After we create such a network over an image, all of its components are fixed with respect to the mesh. Recall that a scene has a large number of DOFs, and we have to determine all of them in a drawing process. This complicated engineering problem can be solved well by triangulation.

Figure 2.27 illustrates how triangulation can lock all DOFs at once. In the figure, we have several shapes of different proportions, orientations, and positions spread out on paper. Each shape has five DOFs in this scene. The triangles created in the figure allow us to confirm all these DOF's values, and the process is quite simple.

You may find that the edges in a triangulation, such as those in Figure 2.27, are very much like the bone structure in a human body. Although a scene generally does not have any anatomical system, a triangulation will be like a virtual skeleton scheme and will help us to conquer each component much more conveniently.

Creating a hierarchical triangulation structure is similar to partitioning polygons (see Figure 2.17) and building a multiresolution representation (see Figure 2.24). The process is simple and easy to follow:

1. Select a small number of key points in a target scene and form a triangulation.

2. Add a few key points to the current triangulation.

3. Repeat step 2 until the structure is fine enough to draw.

The preceding process looks like a computer algorithm. Its simplicity enables anyone to implement it, but I will demonstrate it.

Figure 2.27

A triangulation locks all DOFs.

A *key point* is a point that is used to triangulate the scene. Technically, any point can be used as a key point. However, we typically select from the following candidates: landmarks; intersection points of multiple lines; sharp corners of objects or interesting areas; end points of lines or boundaries; the highest, lowest, leftmost, or rightmost point; and any visually important spots in the scene.

In Figure 2.28, I use black dots to denote key points. The top-left image shows the first step of triangulating, using the same image as in the previous section. I use only a few key points picked from the image, just to lock the area of interest. The top-right image shows the next step: a few more key points (represented by smaller dots) are added, followed by a re-triangulation with the existing dots. The dotted lines in the figure are optional, because they are there only for the sake of triangulation and don't represent any useful visual patterns in the image. In the future, I could omit them so that the triangulation is a collection of polygons instead of triangles. The bottom-left image shows the result of adding some new points. At this moment, the area of interest is covered by several polygons. The bottom-right image is one more level down in the image hierarchy.

The method to extract the GSs in Figure 2.28 is quite simple, but the result is not. Don't be scared by the complexity of the triangulation. What is presented here is a method that will guide you in analyzing and creating a hierarchical triangulation structure. The actual drawing based on this scheme is much simpler—triangulation is not our goal, but it is a method to help us manage graphic information in the image. In the next chapter, I will show you how to use triangulation to draw images with various GSs.

Figure 2.28

Key points (top left) used to lock the area of interest, more key points added (top right), result of adding new points (bottom left), result of one more level down in the image hierarchy (bottom right)

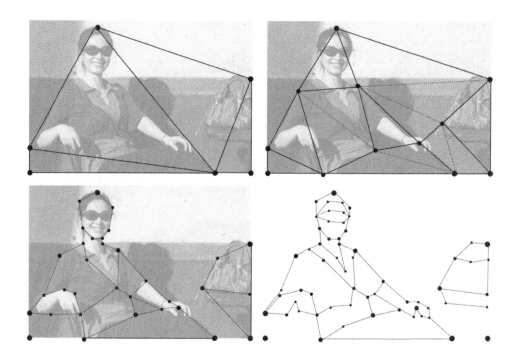

CHAPTER 3

Drawing with the ABC Method

Design is not just what it looks like and feels like. Design is how it works.

—*STEVE JOBS (1955–2011), AMERICAN COMPUTER ENTREPRENEUR AND INVENTOR*

In the previous chapters, you learned how graphics are structured and what kind of information you need to pull out from a scene. You've already read that "learning to draw is learning to see," but this famous quote tells only half the truth. The missing aspect of this quote is "learning to draw structures."

Although knowing how to view objects and obtain useful graphics is important, that understanding does not automatically give us the ability to draw things correctly and efficiently. We must have a way to utilize the information and convert it to graphical elements on paper. In other words, the method for acquiring and the method for drawing should be consistent. Otherwise, different approaches in the two parts of the drawing process might confuse you.

This chapter introduces the angle-based constructive (ABC) method of drawing. Designing a serious drawing method is not as easy as it sounds. As would be the case in the sciences, any new method needs to follow the right principles and meet the desired requirements. So before presenting the basics of the ABC method, I will walk you through the characteristics that make it such a beneficial approach.

Specifically, in this chapter, you will learn about the following topics:

- The criteria fulfilled by the ABC method

- The six basic drawing techniques of the ABC method

Meeting the Criteria for a New Drawing Method

Unlike doodling, drawing realistically is a serious task requiring you to solve multiple challenges simultaneously. As noted earlier in this book, the key to the drawing process is to arrange graphical elements correctly—that is, to put them in the right spots with the correct rotations and proportions.

Although the goal is quite clear, the way to reach such a target is not so obvious. Certainly, many drawing methods have already been developed, and more will appear in the future. Each method may use different guidelines for different purposes or for certain types of objects. As you'll see in this section, the ABC method fulfills the criteria for providing an easy-to-learn, universal tool-free approach to observational drawing.

Must Be Tool-Free

A successful drawing method should be *tool-free*—and by that, I mean no physical *devices* should be used besides a paper and pencil. Implements such as rulers, templates, compasses, and protractors should not be part of an observational drawing method. If there is any "tool" used, it is the drawing *theory* that helps us to complete the job more effectively.

You may wonder why the pencil we grasp for drawing is not considered a tool in this case. Technically, the pencil or anything you hold for drawing *is* a tool, but this tool is acceptable because it is a necessary part of the drawing activity.

As stated in Chapter 1, "Understanding the Relationship between Math and Art," tool-assisted drawing ability is not a real drawing skill even though we have to use some of these devices in special cases. As a general criterion, tool-free drawing forces us to use a method that focuses on solving drawing problems with our bare hands instead of relying on devices.

Requires No Inborn Art Talent

Observational drawing is a basic skill rather than an advanced one. We should never expect anyone to have naturally good drawing abilities. Instead, a low entry-bar should be expected for this basic drawing skill. An ideal scenario is that those who have no art experience can still pick up the method without problems.

Although no innate art ability is needed, every method depends on certain skills such as thinking or analyzing capabilities. You might wonder whether my method based on math and computer graphics will be too hard for the average person to learn without any college-level knowledge in these subjects. The answer is no. Anyone with a middle-school education can easily grasp the principles of this method. Even elementary-school children who have a good understanding of basic geometry concepts (angles, triangles, and so on) should be able to learn this method.

Must Be Simple to Use and Easy to Follow

Learning to draw is a tough job for most people. This is mainly because many are taught some not-so-easy-to-learn methods that are based on using indescribable "feelings" rather than solid principles and easy steps. In order to change this situation, a new method must be simple to use and easy for the average person to follow.

Unlike math, a drawing process does not have a strong sense of sequence. Your pencil can land almost anywhere at any time. Generally speaking, you don't have to sketch objects in any particular order. However, this doesn't mean that order is useless. Without a sequential process, the massive number of options available can frustrate beginners. When students don't know what to do next, they often repeatedly redraw existing lines or doodle in an oblivious manner. A well-organized and standard procedure can fix this problem by guiding people in what to do step-by-step. A method that is clearly designed as a sequence of easy-to-follow actions will flatten the learning curve for beginners.

Traditionally, people tend to draw from top to bottom and from left to right, creating details on paper right away. However, this conventional handwriting order is not very good for managing pictorial information, because planning all structures without a proven strategy is an impossible task for most people. We can solve this problem by arranging graphical structures in a special order and format so that drawing them becomes a sequence of baby steps. Following such a method is key to helping you learn to draw successfully.

The multiresolution organization of graphical structures discussed in the preceding chapter suggests not only that it is possible to organize a complicated scene into layers in a simple hierarchical order but that each layer can be built from the previous layers by using simple operations. The ABC method takes this approach.

Should Be Universally Applicable

We are looking for a way to draw whatever we see realistically, so the method must be general enough to cover all kinds of objects—either 2D or 3D, still life or animals. As you have already learned, the existing perspective theory and the grid method have serious limitations in their application scopes. A good method should overcome this obstacle and work in all observational drawing situations. This is the criterion that inspired me to create the ABC method in order to manipulate spatial structures directly on the picture plane. When we see objects, everything becomes a 2D image on the picture plane. Therefore, extracting these flattened objects and duplicating them on paper provides a universal approach to all types of objects.

In computer graphics, there are usually two distinct approaches to handling graphics information. The first one is working on the target objects—investigating their structures and then using the information for rendering. You may consider all 3D software such as Maya examples of this approach. The second one is directly manipulating the 2D images of the objects on a computer screen. Photoshop takes this approach to process pictures instead of the original objects. In the drawing field, the perspective theory is more like the former style, so it strongly depends on the 3D structures of the target objects. Drawing images on the picture plane is analogous to working on the display without worrying about what kind of scene you have. If you see an oval on the picture plane, you just draw the oval using the properties of the oval. You don't have to work on the original 3D ball or cylinder from which the oval is generated. A method that does not depend on target objects automatically becomes a one-size-fits-all solution.

Provides a Multiresolution Approach with Adaptive Refinement

Graphical structures are not arranged flatly. Instead, they all have different resolutions and can be organized or viewed hierarchically. For better performance, we need to take full advantage of this golden property. By processing information from the big picture down to smaller features, a multiresolution approach not only simplifies the drawing process but also provides a good trade-off for drawing complicated scenes while working under a time constraint. Adding detail selectively and progressively, known as "adaptive refinement," allows an artist to work on the interesting spots without breaking the structure hierarchy.

Modern CG has used this strategy in various applications with great success. There is no reason why we should ignore or reject such a proven process. The ABC method definitely meets this desirable criteria.

Is Based on Proven Theories

Some existing drawing methods were developed from artists' experiments rather than scientific principles. Without strong theoretical support, a method will hardly become a systematic solution. From your point of view, a "just-do-it" method is hard to follow if you do not understand how it works. In addition, observational drawing is an activity that involves lots of logical thinking, in contrast to the popular "right-brain" hypothesis. Therefore, a drawing theory based on scientific principles makes sense as a way for artists to achieve good results. In the history of art methodology, the perspective theory is supported by a 3D math transformation that maps 3D space to 2D space. Therefore, it is not surprising that the theory is so useful in drawing 3D objects, even though it is not a perfect solution. The grid method solves 2D drawing problems with coordinates and tools. Both of these theory-supported methods work well within their limited scopes. The ABC method follows this scientific approach in order to efficiently solve the problem of duplicating shapes from the picture plane to paper.

Is Adaptable to Special Structures

Although a new method should be universally applicable, it should not conflict with any special structures in a target object. Many objects have unique and strong graphic patterns, for example. An ideal drawing method must be able to work naturally with such bonus information. While using the same method for drawing human and animal anatomies and the cubic forms of buildings, the special configurations of these objects will give you additional assistance for drawing them on paper. But not every method has been designed to do so. For example, the contour-line method is an example of ignoring global structural knowledge and focusing on local details only. The negative space method does not take advantage of organization of parts inside the target object (positive space).

Introducing the ABC Method

The criteria listed in the preceding section form the basis for my new drawing solution, the angle-based constructive (ABC) method. This section introduces this method, which provides a systematic approach to observational drawing.

Through this method, you will see a new way to manage graphical structures. First, this section presents the six basic techniques you must learn in order to master the ABC method. The section then provides a brief description of the method, followed by some demonstrations.

Six Basic Drawing Techniques

The following six techniques are core skills, and you must master them in order to learn the ABC method. The six tasks are listed from easy to hard and from a fundamental level to a high level. The latter ones are dependent on the previous ones.

- Estimating angles without devices
- Duplicating a reference line
- Locating points and minimizing errors
- Measuring and controlling proportions
- Duplicating basic shapes
- Assembling shapes

Estimating Angles without Devices

An angle is an essential concept in geometry. However, angles are often not emphasized and have not received the attention they deserve in art books and classes. In the ABC

method, almost everything is based on angles, because angles have many helpful properties that enable us to draw better and faster.

Mathematically, an *angle* is a figure formed by two rays sharing the same vertex, or
point. Angles are measured in degrees. A typical angle ranges from 0 to 180 degrees.
However, you should also become familiar with these special cases: First, when two rays
overlap, they form a 0-degree angle. Second, if the two rays are perpendicular to each
other, a 90-degree angle is constructed. Third, a straight line is technically a 180-degree
angle, but we still view it as a line instead of an angle.

Angles are essential to triangles and polygons in math. For this reason, triangles and
polygons are good tools to work with angles; that is, we will use triangles and polygons
to access angles instead of accessing angles directly. Figure 3.1 illustrates the commonly
used angles existing in a square and an equilateral triangle.

Figure 3.1

Various angles

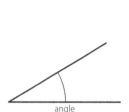
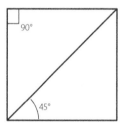
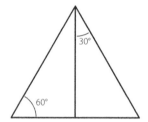

An angle can be measured in two types of units: degrees and radians. The former is widely
used in daily life, and the latter is more popular in math books.

The conversion rate between them is as follows: a full circle has 360 degrees, or 2π radians
(here, $\pi \approx 3.14159$). This relationship gives us 1 radian ≈ 57.2958 degrees.

For simplicity, this book uses degrees. The following information is useful to know
when measuring angles: a right angle is 90 degrees, an equilateral triangle has angles of
60 degrees, and in a square that is cut in half diagonally, the angle between the diagonal line
and an edge of the square is 45 degrees.

Typically, you need a device such as a protractor to accurately measure an angle. But in
freehand drawing, 100 percent accuracy is neither possible nor necessary. Instead, we are
seeking a fast evaluation of angles with decent, but not perfect, accuracy.

Using an imaginary clock is a simple way to quickly estimate angles without using
any devices. This imaginary clock is the old-fashioned, analog type with 12 numbers on
its surface. These numbers divide a circle into 12 equal sections, and each section is a
30-degree angle. Furthermore, many other special angles can be easily found in a clock,
as indicated in Figure 3.2.

Using a clock to indicate directions is popular in the military because of its simplicity.
A soldier may say, "Enemy at 3 o'clock!" to inform comrades about the location of rival

forces, for instance. Some art books, such as Brian Curtis' *Drawing from Observation: An Introduction to Perceptual Drawing* (McGraw-Hill, 2009), also use the clock trick to measure angles. However, this trick is not commonly used in the art community.

If you have difficulty imagining a clock, an alternative solution is to use four fingers to form a quarter of a clock, as shown in Figure 3.3. In this example, the pinky finger would be pointing at 12 on the imaginary clock, and the index finger would be pointing at 3.

Figure 3.2

Angles in a clock

Although angles are a core concept in the ABC method, you won't be calculating the actual values of angles as you learn this new way to draw. Instead, you will be using angles only as a way to help you organize and orient graphical structures. That being said, you are expected to understand angles and familiar with the special angles in Figure 3.1. If you see a line pointing at some up-right direction, you should be able to tell it is close to 1 o'clock or 2 o'clock. Although it seems to be trivial, fast estimating an angle will enable to you do the next five tasks much more efficiently.

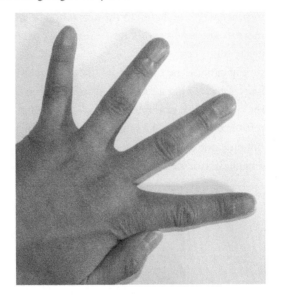

Figure 3.3

Using fingers for angles

Duplicating a Reference Line

A *reference line* is a straight line used to assist your drawing rather than as part of the final drawing. Typically, there are two popular ways to create a line: as a line segment connecting two points or as a ray starting from a vertex and shooting out at a given direction. Both types are useful in drawing. The former is used to link two known locations, and the latter is preferred when we want a line with a certain angle. Figure 3.4 provides an example of both cases.

Figure 3.4

Two popular ways to create a reference line

There are three slightly different math concepts regarding lines: the line segment, ray, and line. A *line segment* has two end points. A *ray* has only one end point and extends infinitely from that point in one direction. A *line* extends infinitely in both directions. In daily life, all we use are line segments. Therefore, you should consider all three concepts interchangeable in this book, unless specified otherwise.

Despite the difference in styles, a reference line is mainly controlled by the angle between the line and a horizontal (or vertical) direction. Therefore, if we want to duplicate a reference line from the picture plane to paper, the key is to copy its angle. In geometric theory, reproducing an angle can be done efficiently without any measurement—by using parallel lines. If two lines are parallel, they must have the same angle measurement in relation to the horizontal or vertical plane. We don't need any tools to measure those angles, because our naked eye is good at catching the parallelism with a pretty high accuracy.

You can use the three sets of lines in Figure 3.5 to test such natural ability. Each pair of lines is enclosed in a rectangle. The left line in each pair is the reference line. The line on the right in each example represents an attempt to duplicate the reference line. All three reference lines have the same angle measurement (60 degrees above the horizontal plane). But only one of the three duplicated lines is truly parallel to its reference line. Most people don't have trouble identifying which pair is perfectly parallel. Try it and see how you do.

Figure 3.5

Test your ability to detect parallel lines.

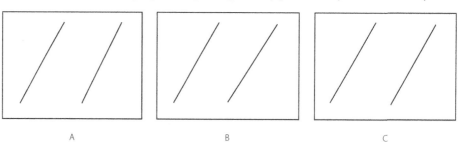

A   B   C

The set of lines marked C is the parallel one. The duplicated line in set A is at 57 degrees above horizontal, and B is at 63 degrees. This test shows how fast and accurate our eyes can be in detecting parallel lines.

Duplicating reference lines without using any devices is a key feature of the ABC method. It gives us a quick and effective solution to draw the lines we desire. It should be pointed out, however, that the paper must be in standing position or close to the vertical direction in order to take advantage of this simple parallel-line trick. Such a paper position is also frequently required in observational drawing. If you cannot set the paper vertically for some reason, it will be much harder for you to duplicate a reference line because you cannot take advantage of the native eye detection ability for parallel lines. In this case, you will mainly use your angle-estimation skill.

Locating Points and Minimizing Errors

Where to put down the pencil on paper is the first important question we encounter in a drawing process. In addition, an essential part of any graphical structure is its position in relation to others.

Traditionally, a point on the paper is uniquely determined by using two coordinates: the point's distance from the left side of the paper and its distance from the bottom. The horizontal and vertical lines in the left image of Figure 3.6 indicate these two distances. This simple technique has been widely used in the grid method and in engineering drawings, but a measuring tool is typically required. Therefore, we need a better solution to replace this old technique.

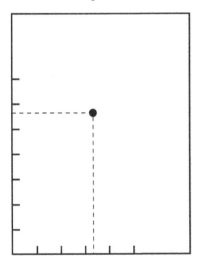 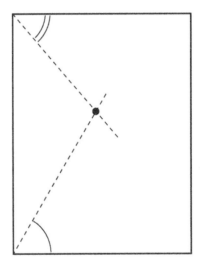

Figure 3.6

Locating a point by using distances (left) and by using reference lines (right)

In geometry, a point has two *degrees of freedom (DOFs)*. In other words, a point is completely determined by two restrictions. Using distance is just one way, but not the only way, to set up these restrictions. A better alternative is to use reference lines or their angles, because a point can be defined as the intersection of two reference lines. The right image of Figure 3.6 shows how two reference lines, one from the top-left corner and the other from the bottom-left corner, intersect at the desired location.

The benefit of using reference lines rather than distances is huge. You don't need tools or any time-consuming steps to measure spatial offsets. To find a point, you just need to create two difference lines containing this point. After getting these two lines, you get the target point as their intersection immediately. Therefore, the parallel-check of reference lines allows us to locate a point efficiently and totally tool-free.

Obviously, the ability to use only our eyes to do a job precisely is an ideal scenario. Although this technique is easy, errors can occur, depending on the individual's observational ability. Therefore, a remedial solution called *multireference checking* can be used. Instead of using only two reference lines to lock the two DOFs, we can use as many reference lines as we want. All fixed points and nearby landmarks can be utilized to create reference lines.

Figure 3.7 shows an example of using four reference lines. Each line comes from a corner of the paper. Theoretically, all these lines should meet at the same location—that is, the place we are looking for. But human drawing errors make each line a little bit off. These displacements instantly result in more than one intersection point among the reference lines. These points are marked by small circles in the figure. Based on statistics theory, the best bet for the desired location is the average of these points. Thus, we can get a pretty accurate spot quickly, indicated by a black dot in the figure, although no tools are used.

Figure 3.7

Multireference checking strategy

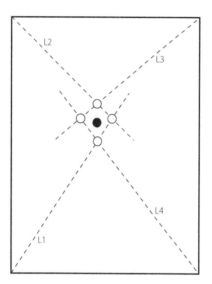

When numerous reference lines are available to pair together for locating a point, you should select a pair of lines that are close to forming a 90-degree angle. The pair L1 and L2 and the pair L1 and L4 in Figure 3.7 are two good examples. If two lines are close to parallel, such as the pair L1 and L3 and the pair L2 and L4, they are bad choices, and you should avoid using them. In these bad pairs, the intersection point is particularly sensitive to line direction, so any tiny error in line direction will cause the intersection to be noticeably off.

Measuring and Controlling Proportions

Measuring and controlling proportions is a major task in drawing. Because of the irregular boundaries of a graphical shape, we typically measure the proportion of its boundary box—that is, the length/width ratio of the rectangle containing the graphical structure.

Currently, *all* observational drawing books teach the technique of using a pencil as a distance-measuring tool to solve proportion problem. For instance, to duplicate a rectangle correctly on paper, you hold a pencil and stretch out that arm in front of you. You then measure the width of the rectangle you see by making a mark on the pencil with your fingertip, as shown in the left image of Figure 3.8. Finally, you use this mark to evaluate the length of the rectangle and finish the task.

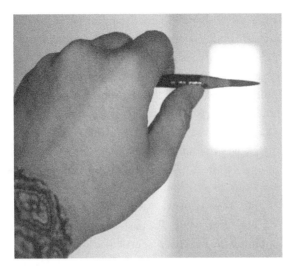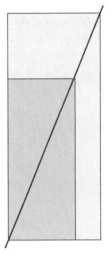

Figure 3.8

Traditional proportion measurement (left) and diagonal-line measurement (right)

Sadly, this measuring process is both error-prone and time-consuming. To measure a ratio, several steps are typically needed, and each of them may introduce errors caused by our physical limitations. Each step is slow and tedious. Even worse, a length/width ratio usually is not a whole number. If a ratio is, say, 2.35 exactly, artists may come up with various approximations—anywhere from 2 to 3—depending on their level of experience. This old technique increases the difficulty of drawing and slows down the process as well. The following is a simple but powerful substitution.

Trigonometry theory tells us that the length/width ratio is uniquely determined by the direction of the diagonal line. If the diagonal line is fixed, all rectangles will have the same ratio regardless of their sizes. The right image of Figure 3.8 shows two rectangles with the same proportions because they share the same diagonal line. In other words, the task of measuring and controlling a proportion is converted into evaluating a diagonal line or its angle. This solution is perfectly consistent with the techniques of duplicating reference lines discussed earlier. You will use this technique throughout this book.

Duplicating Basic Shapes

Graphical structures are made up of simple shapes. The preceding chapter indicated two such geometric elements that are used for the basic shapes in this book: ovals and polygons. Mastering basic shapes is the foundation of learning how to draw. A person must be able to sketch these two shapes well in order to deliver good final artwork.

Sketching a good oval is not easy for inexperienced artists. Part of the reason is that the smoothness and symmetry of an oval make the shape very sensitive to drawing errors—even a tiny mistake will be noticeable. A good way to draw a small-sized oval is to lightly sketch the oval at the same spot again and again, about 5–20 times, as shown in Figure 3.9. A good-looking oval shape will finally appear because each sketch swings near the ideal curve. Surely this task is done by hand-eye coordination ability and thus requires practice to get a high-quality result.

Figure 3.9

Sketching an oval

Drawing a *large* oval without guides is especially challenging. The most difficult part is to control the two ends that people frequently draw either too sharp or too flat. Several methods have been taught in various books to create a large oval, including the following simple way to find individual points on the target oval.

Figure 3.10 illustrates the process. It starts with two circles that share with the same center point O, one small and one big. Their radii are the minor and major radii of the oval to create, respectively. The dash-line represents the target oval. To find a point of the oval near a particular area, just shoot a line from the point O toward that direction (see line OA in Figure 3.10). Assume this line intersects the big circle at A and the intersects small circle at B. Now, draw a vertical line from A and a horizontal line from B. Their intersection point C is what you are looking for; i.e., C is on the oval. Similarly, you can get points D and E with the same simple process. If you find enough such points on the oval, you can sketch the whole oval.

Figure 3.10

Find points on an oval.

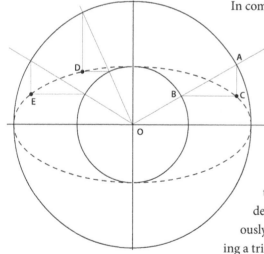

In comparison to drawing an oval, duplicating a polygon is fairly easy because of its linear boundaries. Let's first take a look at the simplest case: a triangle. The key to reproducing a triangle from an observed structure is using parallel lines.

Figure 3.11 shows an example of copying the triangle ABC as the triangle PQR. If we are able to produce lines PQ, QR, and RP so that PQ//AB, QR//BC, and RP//CA, then the triangle PQR is *similar* to ABC. Here the symbol // stands for *parallel*, and the geometry term *similar* guarantees that the generated triangle will resemble the original triangle, regardless of their sizes. Actually, this method strongly depends on the skill of drawing reference lines discussed previously. After you can sketch lines with reasonable accuracy, duplicating a triangle should be an easy job.

In general, there are two methods used to copy polygons. Both take advantage of similar triangles. The first method is to triangulate the polygon so that we can then just duplicate all the triangles in the mesh. After that task is completed, the boundary of the mesh is what we need. Figure 3.12 shows an example of extracting the forehead of a facial structure as a simple polygon. We can duplicate this shape with a few triangles. This method is easy to learn because it is basically a simple process of copying triangles.

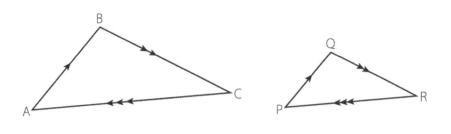

Figure 3.11

Copying a triangle

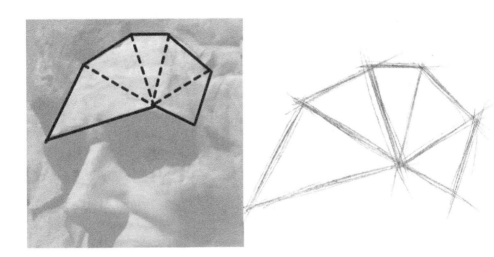

Figure 3.12

Duplicating a simple polygon

However, if a polygon is complicated—that is, it contains many edges—creating and copying a triangle mesh becomes tricky. In this situation, we need to approach the task in a hierarchical way or deconstruct it into smaller pieces or both. Figure 3.13 illustrates the process.

In the top-left image of Figure 3.13, you can see that the eyes and nose form a complicated polygonal shape.

We simplify the original polygon into two simple polygons, as shown at the top right. Then we duplicate them, as shown in the bottom-left image. A refinement step is then executed in order to add more details at the top of these two simple polygons. The bottom-right image shows the result.

You may notice that some anatomy knowledge is used to divide the polygon. Such knowledge is not required for drawing polygons, but it provides some extra help in controlling complicated structures such as the human face.

Figure 3.13

A complicated polygon (top left), polygon simplification (top right), duplicated simple polygons (bottom left), and refinement to get the desired result (bottom right)

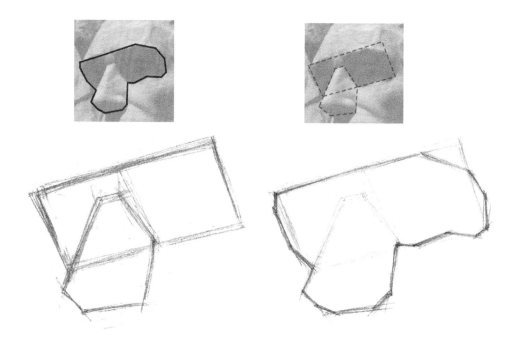

Using polygons as a basic shape provides us with a flexible way to improve drawing skills. Beginners can always subdivide a polygon into triangles and then copy each triangle to restore the polygon (as shown earlier in Figure 3.12). Experienced users can draw a polygon directly without triangulation, as shown in the bottom-left image of Figure 3.13. The benefit of doing the latter is obvious—you can speed up the process and skip the additional steps after your skills have advanced.

Assembling Shapes

Assembling all structures together properly is a core part of the drawing process. You have to take care of positions, orientation, and proportions of all individual items. Although most people can draw simple shapes without too much difficulty, arranging multiple shapes with correct spatial relationships between them can be extremely hard. Artists usually acquire this skill through practice. But let's use your knowledge of graphical structures from the preceding chapter to make the job easier to learn.

Recall that a scene with multiple objects requires us to determine all DOFs. The DOF analysis scientifically demystifies the fact that drawing is a highly complicated task, and we must provide intelligent solutions to deal with it. Unfortunately, and for unknown reasons, almost all art books skip this step and don't teach you how to orient objects. In a typical demonstration, an author will draw multiple objects in a single step on paper without explaining how the objects are arranged. The left image of Figure 3.14 illustrates such a scenario in which several basic shapes are magically sketched. The next step you see is a detailed drawing, as shown in the right image of the figure. This kind of demonstration makes drawing much more difficult to learn, because the most important step, determining locations and proportions, is missing. A beginner can easily get stuck here.

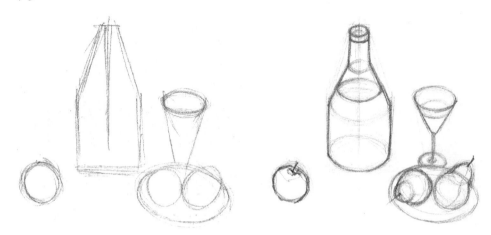

Figure 3.14

Basic shapes are sketched without explanations (left), and detail is added directly (right).

In the preceding chapter, you saw that a good way to solve the DOF problem is triangulation. After objects *and* the space between them are filled with triangles, the whole scene can be viewed as a single, complicated object instead of random items scattered throughout the scene. The left image of Figure 3.15 shows four simple objects on a table and the triangles that "glue" them together like a single entity. Obviously, assembling these objects requires nothing but duplicating the triangulation.

Unlike a computer, the average person cannot easily handle hundreds or even dozens of triangles. Drawing a large number of triangles directly is not practical. Similar to the treatments we used for duplicating polygons, a multiresolution approach is a good strategy to solve this issue.

The center image of Figure 3.15 shows a simple coarse mesh over the objects. This low-resolution triangulation allows us to quickly copy the overall structure of the scene, even though it looks more like a random web. After this big picture is settled, we just need to insert new points progressively. The right image of Figure 3.15 is the result of adding a few new vertices in the mesh with a re-triangulation. This refinement process continues until all graphical structures are well-defined on paper.

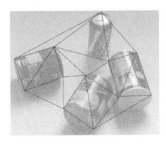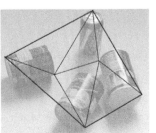

Figure 3.15

A scene and its triangulation (left), a coarse level of the triangulation (center), and a refinement treatment (right)

Regarding this final technique of integrating objects, a triangulation connects all structures in a scene by using a network of lines. This network acts as a skeleton of the scene, but it is not the only solution. For example, we could connect the centers of individual objects to create a virtual anatomical framework (see Figure 3.16). This approach is similar to the *stick figures* used to express essential body anatomy.

Figure 3.16

Connecting the centers of individual objects to create a virtual anatomical framework

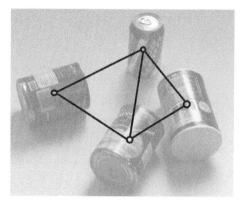

Assembling objects is the most problematic technique because of its complexity. To make solid products, it is necessary to talk about some efficient yet simple tactics to identify and correct mistakes. The first one is using grouped graphical structures—that is, merging selected individual shapes to form a larger one to confirm their spatial relationship. The left image of Figure 3.17 shows two such structures displayed with highlighting. This kind of structure is usually large and thus is easy to identify. Another quick way to validate spatial relationships is by shooting reference lines from key points. The right image of Figure 3.17 demonstrates several reference lines constructed from key point A. The horizontal line (shown as a dashed line) can be used to confirm whether another object is above or below this location, while the other three reference lines directly connect point A with key positions of other objects.

Figure 3.17

Using grouped graphical structures (left) and using reference lines (right)

 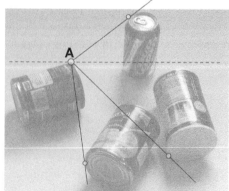

Description of the ABC Method

All six of the preceding techniques really depend on angle control. With these basic techniques mastered, you should have no problem understanding and learning the key concept of this book: the angle-based constructive method.

The ABC method uses angles as a foundation to support various tool-free operations using shapes. This approach seeks to improve real drawing ability by using scientific principles. For teachers, the ABC method makes drawing more teachable because the whole process has detailed instructions and explanations. Every step in this method is constructive and has a clear purpose. For students, drawing becomes much easier because the new method provides a universal and systematic approach to all kinds of graphical structures. All drawing steps can be executed without requiring a high degree of hand-eye coordination ability.

Advanced math or science knowledge is not required to learn this method, but it is of course helpful. Because of the heavy usage of angles, lines, and triangles, you must become familiar with these geometric concepts, which you should have been taught in elementary school.

The ABC method can be described in the following simple steps:

1. For a drawing target (either a 3D scene or 2D image), select several key points or landmarks from the target to form a coarse triangulation or polygon.

2. Duplicate the polygon or triangulation.

3. Pick a few of the more visually important points from the target scene, and add them to the current drawing. Re-triangulation might be needed to ensure the desired degree of accuracy. Repeat this refinement step until all the structures are locked, except for the details.

4. Draw detailed features to finish the artwork.

The ABC method is mainly a sequence of two different operations: selecting key points and duplicating or refining triangles/polygons. The key point selection process may vary from one person to another. That does not matter very much, as long as the points selected are considered to be important or interesting to the person who is doing the drawing.

Step 2 seems to be a little bit tricky because most reference lines exist virtually on the imaginary picture plane. When you duplicate these virtual lines on paper, you have to imagine their existence. In the demonstrations in the rest of this book, I will intentionally display these virtual lines on some of the original pictures in order to help you better understand the process. But such lines will not be displayed for you later to simulate a real observational drawing scenario. A good practice to master triangle duplicating is to add key points progressively. Beginning artists may add one point at a time, while a more experienced individual can add multiple points at once.

Whenever inserting a new point, at least two reference lines are required to pinpoint the location. Extra reference lines are helpful to confirm and adjust the location. Technically, all established points can be used for reference purposes. But these points have different degrees of influence. Generally speaking, the earlier a point is added, the more important the point will be. Therefore, use the earliest-added points as much as possible.

Demonstrations

This section presents four basic demonstrations of the ABC method of drawing. I will draw still-life objects, 2D images, a 3D head, and quick figure sketches. You don't need to draw here as I will guide you learn the method in detailed steps starting from the next chapter.

Various point-selecting and triangulation treatments are described through these demonstrations, but the main drawing approach remains the same. I always draw objects hierarchically and control spatial relationships with angle-based reference lines, triangles, and polygons.

Demo 1: Still-Life Objects

In this demo, I will draw the vase of flowers shown in the top-left image of Figure 3.18. Because the target scene is made up of two kinds of objects, a vase and a flower, it is natural to separate them and approach each with a simple polygon. I drew a small number of points on the outskirts of the scene and then created two such polygons in this case. I then duplicated the polygons with some reference confirmations in the bottom-left image of Figure 3.18. This finishes steps 1 and 2.

Next, because of the complexity of the flowers, we need to partition the polygon further into smaller regions by selecting some key points and copying these subpolygons/meshes on paper. The top-center and bottom-center images of Figure 3.18 show this step, which corresponds to step 3 of the ABC method. Up to this step, there are several small regions on the paper, and each contains some simple graphical structures. I could slice these polygons one more time to simplify each region, but that is not necessary because each flower can be approximated by a simple shape (rectangle, oval, or triangle) pretty quickly inside the subdivided regions, as indicated by the top-right image of Figure 3.18.

Figure 3.18

Initial polygons (top left), refinement (top center), simple shapes to control details (top right), duplicated polygons (bottom left), duplicated partitioning (bottom center), and all details added (bottom right)

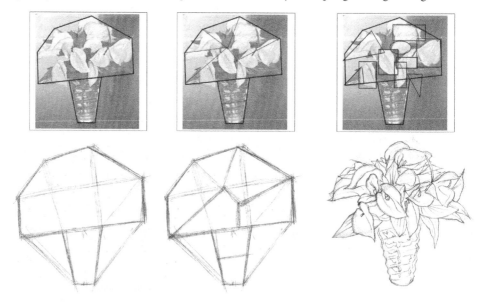

The final step is to duplicate every flower, guided by the polygons/meshes established so far. The bottom-right image of the figure shows the finished work. You might think the last step is quite complicated at first glance. However, each detailed flower is a pretty simple shape. Because the polygonal framework in the previous step locks their positions and sizes, adding the individual flowers is pretty straightforward.

The drawings shown here are all enhanced with Photoshop in order to be visible. However, all sketches (polygons and reference lines) except the final step should be done on paper very lightly so that I won't even have to erase them after the work is complete.

In drawing organic objects such as flowers or the human body, you often must sketch rounded curves instead of sharp-cornered polygons. In this case, using straight lines is less efficient than using slightly curved ones. You will learn more about curved triangles in Chapter 7, "Advanced Techniques." For now, I will use them in upcoming demos in order to illustrate the power of the ABC method.

Demo 2: 2D Images/Artwork

Next, I will duplicate an existing (2D) artwork. As discussed in previous chapters, 2D artwork is different from a 3D scene. I cannot apply perspective theory here in general because the image to copy can be a nonrealistic painting. The most important task is to identify key graphical structures and arrange them hierarchically in order to draw them on paper.

Let me use one of Van Gogh's self-portraits for this demonstration. The original work is an oil painting. I have converted it into a line drawing for this demonstration. The top-left image of Figure 3.19 is the one we will copy.

This time, you will not see the virtual partition lines step-by-step on the original source image. You should be able to see all triangulation information in the drawing steps. The top-center image of Figure 3.19 is the result of drawing a few simple polygons that serve as a coarse mesh.

Because this is a portrait, I can immediately use some common anatomical knowledge to establish spatial relationships between structures on the face. In the top-right image, I draw the eye-line, nose-line, mouth-line, and centerline to quickly capture the arrangement of important facial features. For those who haven't studied anatomy yet, skipping these lines definitely will slow down the whole process. Technically, however, creating a few more triangles will also solve the problem. This example shows that understanding the structures of objects helps us draw better and faster.

The bottom-left image of Figure 3.19 shows more local refinements in the facial area, where I am most interested. The bottom-center image is the final result that is obtained by adding detailed, small structures based on our triangulation.

Figure 3.19

Picture to copy (top left), starting polygons (top center), anatomical knowledge used (top right), further partitioning (bottom left), final result (bottom center), and more dynamic connections (bottom right)

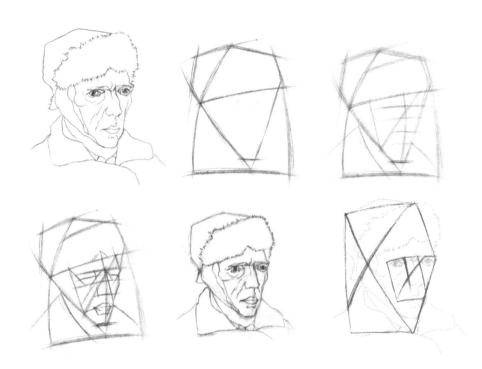

In this drawing, I used some (curved) reference lines to connect disconnected components such as the hat and shoulder. Such virtual links are not based on logic but rather on visual patterns. Being able to identify and use such highly dynamic connections is a key skill used in the ABC method. We can link any two structures together if they provide useful reference lines or special shapes to help us draw better and faster. You will be introduced to various techniques to identify and create dynamic shapes in the coming chapters. The bottom-right image of Figure 3.19 shows some more examples of such virtual and dynamic connections found in this portrait.

Demo 3: A 3D Head

The next demonstration shows how the ABC method works on a 3D head. Technically, there is no major difference between a 3D head and 2D portrait because the ABC method is working on flat images of the picture plane.

I could use anatomical knowledge to help in controlling shapes in this drawing, but I would rather apply a polygon partition to show the power of polygonal shapes and reference lines. The top-left image of Figure 3.20 shows a picture of the original 3D model Planes of the Head, which was designed to train artists how to draw human heads. The head is a kind of 3D polygon model that contains many flat surfaces, so it is fairly easy to extract lines and connect them to form (curved) polygons. After I complete the big polygons, it takes only a few additional partitions to simplify the drawing into simple regions. Then the final details can be drawn quickly.

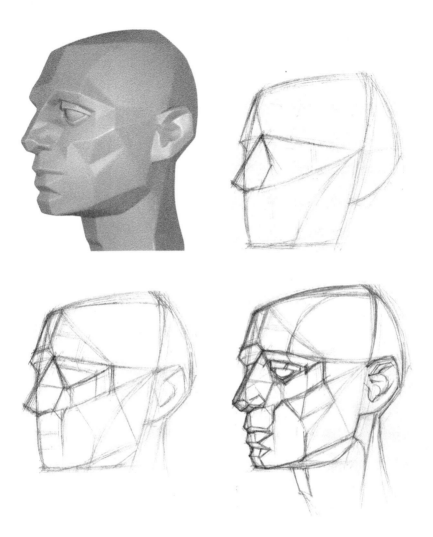

Figure 3.20
3D head to draw
(top left), simple
polygons to start
(top right), more
polygons generated
(bottom left), and
detail added (bot-
tom right)

Demo 4: Quick Figure Sketches

The quick figure sketch is probably the most difficult observational drawing because of the time limit and the complexity of dynamic poses. Unlike the preceding demos, a quick sketch allows no time to create the various levels of polygons. However, the basic principle of the ABC method still holds: identifying and drawing big structures before adding details.

The left image of Figure 3.21 is a 1-minute life figure drawing. In this sketch, only a few coarse polygons are quickly sketched before the detailed lines are immediately added on top of this big framework. The right image of Figure 3.21 recaptures the missing framework in this drawing.

Figure 3.21

A figure quick sketch (left) and simple polygons used to guide drawing of details (right)

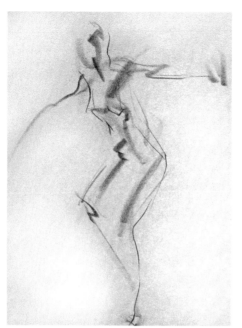 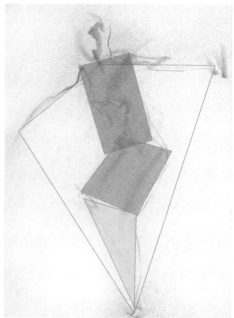

Drawing a quick sketch is a really challenging task for beginners. Chapter 8, "Using Special Tricks on Drawing Human Bodies," covers this further.

So far, you have studied a new method that makes drawing easier to learn and that can be applied to all subjects. This method was developed as a universal freehand solution for observational drawing, overcoming the major scope limitations of other drawing methods. More important, this method proves that the left side of the brain is very helpful to learning art and that our education system needs to adopt a new direction in teaching students to integrate art and science.

CHAPTER 4

Drawing Simple Objects

The journey of a thousand miles begins with one step.

—Lao Tze, Chinese philosopher and founder of Taoism

After learning about various theories for a few chapters, you are probably eager to grab a pencil and paper and begin to draw. Yes, it is time now to roll up your shirtsleeves and have fun with hands-on exercises. As when learning math, you will start with simple individual objects in this chapter, taking one small step at a time and gradually advancing to more-complicated tasks in the coming chapters.

Although the focus of this book is to provide a scientific method for drawing, it is practice that enables you to turn all that knowledge into actual artistic skills. Principles will help you learn how to draw more efficiently, but they are never meant to replace hands-on exercises. So even if you completely understand the theories covered up to this point, you still need to take the time to practice them.

The demonstrations and exercises in this book are designed to help you master basic observational drawing skills step-by-step. I strongly suggest that you follow the chapter order if you are a beginner. If you are already an experienced artist, you can skip some easy exercises, but a quick reading of the text is still preferred to make sure that you are familiar with some of the new techniques presented.

The topics covered in this chapter are as follows:

- **Extracting graphical information**

- **Drawing various simple objects**

Preparing to Draw

Before you officially start practicing with this book, there are a couple of things you need to address. First, you need to set your drawing board in a fairly vertical position instead of laying it down on a table horizontally. Putting the board on an easel or laying it against the back of a chair is an easy solution. Such a setup is also suggested by other observational drawing books, but it is *required* in this book because we mainly use parallel lines to control angles and corresponding shapes. When the paper is parallel to the (vertical) picture plane, it will be easier to compare a line in the picture plane to a line on your paper (see Figure 4.1). Otherwise, judging parallel lines becomes difficult, especially for beginners.

Figure 4.1

Your paper needs to be placed vertically.

The second suggestion is about the darkness of reference lines. You will draw many reference lines during the drawing process. Most of these lines will not be a part of the final product. Therefore, you need to draw them lightly. Inexperienced artists tend to draw every line heavily. You could use an eraser to remove unwanted lines later. But a better solution is to sketch all reference lines as lightly as possible, making them just dark enough to be visible. Avoiding the use of erasers limits the chances of making your drawing messy. It should be noted that all drawing demos in this book are enhanced by software in order to make the reference lines more visible. The actual reference lines are barely visible on paper. Only the final lines are drawn firmly and heavily.

Extracting Basic Information

Recall that there are two major processes in observational drawing: extracting useful graphical information from the scene and drawing basic shapes on paper. These two steps are almost equally critical and are strongly connected. The former identifies geometric structures and associated spatial relationships, while the latter depends on the former and delivers the final artwork.

In this section, you will learn some basic techniques to identify and obtain information necessary for your drawing. An image on the picture plane may contain large numbers of pictorial features. As a result, you must identify what you want to draw and collect the associated information. Because the ABC method takes a hierarchical approach to process graphics anatomically, you need to learn how to obtain general "anatomical" information from a given scene. In particular, you must learn how to select key points, how to determine angles, how to create reference lines, how to generate basic shapes, and how to gather spatial connections between objects.

Identifying Key Points

Key points, as introduced in Chapter 2, "Extracting Graphical Structures—A Scientific Point of View," are used to define triangulations for the image. These key points are like joints or landmarks in human anatomy. By using key points, you can dynamically partition a complicated scene into a group of simple ones before drawing each piece. Because a triangulation is made up of reference lines and each reference line consists of two key points, the fundamental part of this construction chain is nothing but key points.

When you sit in front of a scene, you may find that a lot of points could be used as key points. How should you select them and in what order? Is there any principle for the selection?

A simple guideline to remember is that the purpose of key points is to help in constructing reference lines and later in drawing shapes. Therefore, the criterion for selecting a key point is the structural significance of that point—that is, how important the point is for creating graphical structures. When you have many candidates from which to choose, ask yourself a question: "Which one is more important to help me subdivide the image in order to draw it correctly?"

Here is a list of candidates for key points based on their intrinsic structural influences:

- Extreme points (leftmost, rightmost, top, and bottom points) of a structure
- Landmarks on an object
- Intersection points for existing lines
- End points of existing lines
- Sharp corners of boundary lines
- Merging points of multiple objects
- Special virtual points such as the center of a circle

Figure 4.2 shows various key points in two examples. In the first example, black dots represent extreme points, gray dots are used as landmarks, and hollow circles show intersections of existing lines. A circle with a cross in the first example indicates a special virtual point. In the second example, black triangles mark the end points of existing lines, gray triangles indicate sharp corners, and hollow triangles denote the merging points of objects. Be aware that some points could have multiple features among those listed here. Remember, such points should have important structural value for your drawing.

Figure 4.2

Examples of key points

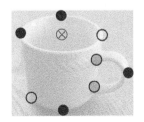

Figure 4.3

Examples of key points

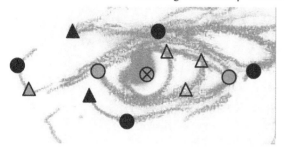

Figure 4.3 is a zoomed-in image of the right side of Figure 4.2; it is another example of marking various key-values. All markers have the same meanings as in Figure 4.2.

Please be aware that there are usually more key points in an image than we need in drawing. That means you don't have to use all such points. You use them only when you need. Another thing you need to watch out for are those virtual key points that don't visually exist in the scene or image. It is much harder to use such imaginary points than actual points. If possible, you can use alternatives. For example, the corners of a bounding box surrounding an object are often invisible in an image. You can use the extreme points instead, as shown in Figures 4.2 and 4.3.

Finding Reference Lines

In most cases, a *reference line* is formed by connecting two *existing* key points. Technically, you can create a reference line simply by linking any two key points, but for the sake of drawing efficiency, you should create and utilize reference lines in any way that achieves the best structural benefits. Because of the many possibilities for determining reference lines, you need to consider some optimization strategies. For the purpose of better structure control, here are some good candidates for choosing reference lines (not an exclusive list):

- Actual lines in the image that look important such as boundaries of objects
- Virtual lines that have special angles—such as vertical, horizontal, diagonal, and parallel lines—or lines merging at vanishing points
- Virtual lines that form good basic shapes
- Virtual lines that connect two important key points
- Virtual lines at a spot where you want to obtain additional information

Figure 4.4 shows samples of these five types of reference lines in a scene.

As you can see, a reference line is not too hard to find if you have selected the correct key points. However, the ABC method also uses reference lines to *allocate* key points. You might wonder which one comes first. This seems to be a chicken-and-egg problem. Here is the order: you identify key points on the picture plane, and then you select reference lines by connecting key points on that plane. These two steps are done in the extracting stage. Next, you move to the drawing stage, where you allocate key points on paper by duplicating those reference lines.

Figure 4.4

Existing lines (top left), vertical and horizontal lines (top right), lines forming basic shapes (middle), lines connecting key points (bottom left), and reference lines at an interesting spot (bottom right)

Obtaining Polygonal Shapes via Simplification

Shapes are the elements we want to produce in our artwork. To make drawing easier and to fit a triangulation strategy, you need to use only two basic shapes in your drawing: polygons and ovals. These shapes are indeed easy for beginners to draw. However, obtaining the associated information from a scene is not trivial.

In Chapter 2, several graphical structures (GSs) were introduced: static, dynamic, individual, grouped, and multiresolution. Although these GSs have different features and purposes, their extracting methods are the same. You use reference lines and key points to obtain all spatial information through a triangulation process. You then keep adding key points until the triangulation or the collection of reference lines enables you to control all of the GSs you want.

With the triangulation strategy, you basically approximate all kinds of GSs with polygons and ovals. In most cases, you will find that polygons are used far more frequently than ovals. Therefore, it is important to learn how to use polygons to approach different GSs. First, it is important to understand that all curves can be approximated by polygons. This simple fact is taught in most art books. In this book, however, you have learned not only how to simplify a curve with polygons but also how to approach it with different resolutions for better control. It is fairly simple to get polygons at different resolutions by dropping less important points in an existing polygon. Figure 4.5 demonstrates a sequence of polygons derived from a GS (face outline).

Figure 4.5

Original polygon (left), simplified polygon (center), and further simplified version (right)

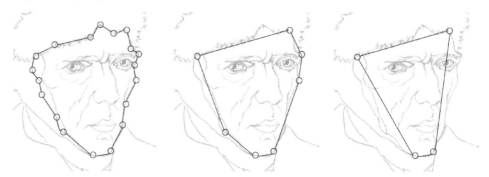

This multiresolution representation of a polygon will simplify your drawing process. For a complicated GS, you can always duplicate it on paper by starting with the simplest version of its polygon approximation and then gradually adding points to reach the full resolution. In this case, you break down the drawing complexity into multiple easy steps.

Obtaining Oval Information

Because an oval is fully controlled by its two axes and the ratio of radii, extracting an oval is simply a matter of determining its axes and the proportions of length and width.

Figure 4.6

Ovals in a cup

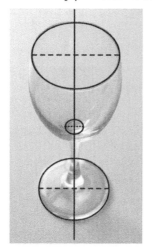

Unfortunately, neither task is easy. The main reason is that an oval is too smooth. Besides its extreme points, it is hard to mark and use any other points on an oval as references. In general, our eyes can pinpoint a corner point easily, but not a point on a smooth surface.

The good news is that most of the time, an oval appears as a cross section of a cylinder or cone (for example, as part of a bottle or cup). The major axis is perpendicular to the center axis of the cylinder or cone. Therefore, acquiring the axis information is relatively easy. Figure 4.6 shows a glass that is part of a cone shape. Three ovals are marked, and their major axes are displayed with dashed lines. The solid vertical line is the axis of the cone hidden within the glass.

However, finding the ratio of radii is typically a hard job. Theoretically, the ratio of radii equals the ratio of the length and width of the bounding box (see Figure 4.7). However, the bounding box is purely virtual. In other words, the vertices of the bounding box are completely imaginary (displayed as hollow circles in the figure). Without physical existence, such points are hard for our eyes to register and trace.

Here is a math solution that solves the problem somewhat, though not perfectly. For a target oval, we first find its two axes and obtain their intersection points with the curve. These are the four points marked by black dots in Figure 4.7. Obviously, these four points form a diamond shape and already determine the ratio of the oval underneath. But for the sake of easily duplicating the oval in the drawing stage, we want to find the direction of the diagonal line of the oval. In Chapter 3, using this direction to measure and control bounding box proportion is one of six techniques on which the ABC method relies. The dashed line in Figure 4.7 shows one of the two diagonal lines of the bounding box. This diagonal line is parallel to two edges of the diamond. In other words, both pairs of the parallel edges in the diamond can be used to control the proportion of the oval. Compared with constructing the bounding box with four corners, this diamond approach does not use any virtual points. All four vertices of the diamond are real points on the oval and easy to track by eye.

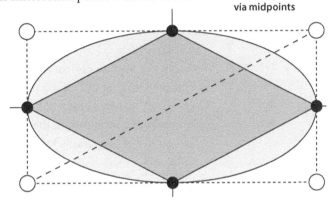

Figure 4.7

Acquiring the ratio via midpoints

Frankly speaking, this math trick is of limited help because our eyes cannot easily identify the points on an oval. Therefore, I recommend that you eyeball the oval you are drawing to *confirm* the aspect ratio when actually drawing it. If the target oval has any obvious marks such a shadow line or a shining reflection spot, you should create a reference to them for further assistance.

The acquisition techniques covered in this section are very basic. More-advanced techniques are explained, along with examples, in Chapter 7 ("Using Advanced Techniques"). Next you will see some demonstrations of simple individual objects that apply the techniques that have already been covered.

Demonstrations of 3D Objects

Learning to draw is just like learning any other subject. We always start with simple cases and gradually move toward complex ones. In this section, you will learn how to draw simple 3D objects, from easy to hard. 2D is covered in the next section. By watching how graphical information is extracted from a scene and then captured on paper, you will see how the ABC method works for all kinds of structures. At the same time, I strongly suggest that you think about how an object is analyzed for its structure, how this information is obtained and organized, and, finally, how to turn geometric data into shapes and draw them on paper.

The ABC method treats all 3D scenes as images on the picture plane, and it uses the same approach to draw a 2D picture of a real object. Because of the limitations of a printed book page, all demos of 3D objects in this section are explained by using their *pictures,* and you will have to draw from these instead of viewing the real 3D objects. But you will learn the techniques that truly apply to both 3D and 2D objects.

Although we use the same method to extract graphical information from the picture plane for all kinds of objects, there is a minor difference between 2D and 3D objects when you observe them. You have to flatten a 3D scene in your mind when you are facing a real object. A beginner might find this difficult. Closing one eye is the traditional artists' approach to making everything flat, because doing so removes depth information from the object. A flattened object still looks 3D because of shading, but it appears as in a giant 2D photo before your eyes. In the case of drawing a 2D image, the flat image is exactly what is on the picture plane. No flattening is needed.

AN OBJECT WITH OR WITHOUT DEPTH INFORMATION

With both of your eyes open, you can sense the depth of an object in front of you because each eye captures a slightly different picture of the object. Our brain can perceive the distance between you and the object based on these two pictures. If only one eye is open, you cannot sense the object's depth anymore.

One simple experiment is to place a small object (say, a coin) on a table in front of you. With both eyes open, you can accurately put your index finger a couple of inches right above the coin and move it down vertically to touch the coin. But doing so with only one eye open will be extremely hard, because you cannot sense the depth of the coin this time. Because of this missing depth information, you cannot judge the true 3D distance between your finger and the coin based only on their 2D images on the picture plane.

All 3D objects for the demonstrations in this section are regular items that exist in the real world. Therefore, after you draw each image by following the instructions provided, it is a good idea to draw real ones by yourself.

Spherical Objects

There are many spherically structured items in our lives, such as eggs, oranges, and baseballs. A ball always appears spherical, no matter how we look at it. Therefore, we don't need to determine its orientation and scales.

Drawing a ball without any textures on its surface wouldn't be very interesting, so I selected a beach ball for this demo. The ball has some cross-section circles on its surface (see the left image of Figure 4.8). These circles appear as ovals in the perspective view, as indicated by the center image of Figure 4.8. The key part of this drawing is to sketch these ovals in their correct relationships inside a circle.

 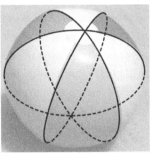 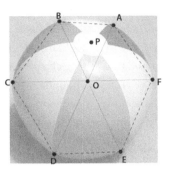

Figure 4.8

Beach ball (left), ovals in the ball (center), and reference lines (right)

You can see that the ovals intersect the boundary of the ball at six points. These points, marked A through F, are the points on the ovals' major axes (see the right image of Figure 4.8). Therefore, they are perfect as key points. Additionally, reference lines AD, BE, and CF pass through the center of the ball, O, according to the principles of geometry. These tips are useful in helping us to reproduce the six points on a sketched circle (see the left image of Figure 4.9).

 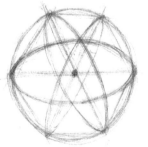 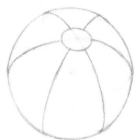

Figure 4.9

Duplicating key points and reference lines (left), sketching ovals (center), and the final result (right)

Obviously, you can further use reference lines such as AB, BC, CD, and so forth, to confirm and correct the locations of the six points on paper. Feel free to use the parallel-line technique when you duplicate reference lines.

Another key point, P, is located near the center of triangle ABO. The point P is a virtual intersection of all three ovals. After marking P on paper, you can then lightly sketch the three ovals (see the center image of Figure 4.9). So far, every single line on the paper should be drawn lightly because they are just sketches instead of the final lines. Images displayed in Figure 4.9 are intensity-enhanced for you to see. These sketching lines should be so light that you might not need to erase them after you draw the final lines (see the right image of Figure 4.9).

Boxlike Objects

Boxlike objects are probably the most popular man-made structures. From books and tables to automobiles and buildings, we see them almost everywhere. Being able to draw boxes is an essential skill for general observational drawing.

Drawing a boxlike object seems to be easy because of its simple structure and straight boundaries. The tricky part, however, is determining the angles of edges. A box contains three groups of boundary lines in 3D space. Each group has four parallel lines. According to the perspective theory, these parallel lines may not remain parallel in the picture plane, depending on the directions of the parallel lines. The traditional perspective drawing sets up horizontal lines and various vanishing points on paper in order to determine the angles of these boundary edges. Such a tedious process can be replaced by a true angle duplication operation in the ABC method.

Figure 4.10 shows a tissue box that sits in front of us at a fairly close range. The short range causes some noticeable distortion of boundary edges due to the perspective transformation. The center image of Figure 4.10 displays the three groups of "parallel lines" with different line styles (solid, thin, and dotted) in a perspective view. At this particular angle, the vertical lines are distorted heavily, while the other lines are distorted only slightly. If we extend these lines to obtain their vanishing points, they are clearly off the paper. This example demonstrates the advantage of duplicating angles instead of using vanishing points in these types of cases. We don't have to create a perspective system to reproduce these lines.

Obviously, all visible corners of the box should be selected as key points. The silhouette of the box is a hexagon, and it can be partitioned with reference lines connecting any pair of key points. In the right image of Figure 4.10, solid lines are edges of the box, and dotted lines represent various reference lines available to verify the spatial relationship among key points. Surely, you don't have to use all these reference lines, but they are handy, supportive tools. Without using them, you may end up drawing the box too long or too thin. The hexagon is highlighted for your convenience to see this box in 2D format.

Figure 4.10

Tissue box (left), distorted edges (center), and reference lines (right)

The left image of Figure 4.11 shows a sketch of the box and some reference lines.

If you're a beginner who finds it too hard to draw a hexagon when employing reference lines, you can sketch the box from one rectangle face to another, which makes it much easier. The right side of Figure 4.11 is the final drawing of the box shape.

This demonstration is meant to show you how to duplicate an observed box structure. Other details such as the tissue, open hole, and textures are not important at this time. They are ignored to avoid complicating the exercise.

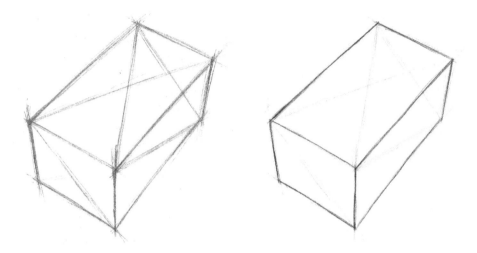

Figure 4.11

Duplicating key points with reference lines (left) and the final drawing of the box (right)

Cylinder or Cone-Based Objects

Many items are composed of cylinder or cone structures. Cups, pencils, bottles, and even human arms, just to name a few, consist of these structures. The major difference between a cylinder and a cone is their profiles. From the side, a cylinder looks like a rectangle, and a cone looks like a triangle. A cylinder keeps its thickness unchanged, but a cone tapers at one end. The common feature of these two structures is a circular cross section. Actually, many ovals that we view daily are cross sections of cylinders or cones.

In this demonstration, a cone-based cup is the target object (see Figure 4.12). This object seems to be a little more complicated because of the handle and some surface decorations, but the main body is just part of a cone. To draw this cup, you need to determine its length and the proportions for the ovals on the top and the bottom of the cup. The center image of Figure 4.12 shows a few of the key points selected from the two ovals by using their extreme vertices. To control the height of the cup, a diagonal reference line is indicated here. Based on this simple fact, a sketch using a quadrilateral can be easily created, as you'll see later in this section in Figure 4.13.

In order to acquire important information about the ovals, some more key points need to be added. These points are the extreme vertices of the ovals. The handle is a small-sized ring structure, and a couple of key points are enough to secure its size and position (see the rightmost image of Figure 4.12). The power of key points is their flexibility in connecting with each other, although we usually connect contiguous points instead of more-distant ones. From the image, you can see that the reference lines form a skeleton structure for the cup. All geometric information is determined by these key points and reference lines. That is why we select the most influential key points and identify the most useful reference lines.

Although reference lines are extremely useful for solving spatial issues, not every reference line is easy to use. If a reference line is also an existing line, such as line CE in Figure 4.12, it is pretty easy to use. But most of the time, a reference line is imagined. Such a line does not exist in the scene, nor can we draw it in the imaginary image plane. In this case, beginners may have difficulty "seeing" such nonexistent lines and will draw them by using parallel checks. This part is probably the most challenging task in the ABC method, and it surely requires practice to master it.

Figure 4.13 shows four snapshots of the process of drawing the cup.

Simplified Complicated Objects

Figure 4.13

Sketching the main part (left), drawing reference lines and key points (center left), sketching all parts (center right), and the final drawing (right)

This section covers complicated objects that you can draw by simplifying them. The level of simplification depends on how much detail you *want* to draw or how much time you are *allowed* to draw. For instance, when you look at a tree, it contains hundreds of thousands of leaves. No artist wants to draw all of these small graphics one by one. Instead,

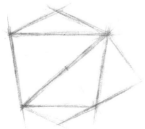

artists often simplify a tree into a cone shape or a few winding lines representing the tree's overall appearance.

Simplification is a powerful tool for artists, and you should master it. Any object can have a lot of detail. Even a blank, white sheet of paper has innumerable tiny microstructures when you put it under a microscope. But we never draw them because our eyes cannot see them. When you look at a large object such as a tree, you may see many small features. Beginners often focus their attention on the details and forget the overall picture. That mind-set makes drawing harder than it should be. Professional artists usually simplify such objects into basic shapes so that the drawing process is easier to control.

How do you simplify a complicated object? Well, there are several ways to do this. A naive approach would be to back away from the object until you don't see any detail other than the overall shape. A high-tech tactic is to shrink a large picture of an object down to a thumbnail size so that the details vanish. A smarter way, however, is to *ignore* the details and pay attention to only the most important features or shapes. In the demonstration of the tissue box, you already saw how we ignored the tissue and the busy textures painted on the box, because we didn't need to draw them in order to complete the basic shape.

Simplification is therefore a bridge between simple objects and complicated objects. I consider a polygon *complicated* if it has more than six sides. You might hold a slightly different opinion on this matter, depending on your skills. But whether your bar is set to a 20-gon or a triangle, it does not matter. You just need to reduce a complicated object into a simple one that you are then able to control. By following this rule, you can conquer any object.

In this demonstration, you will view a complicated object but draw it as a simple one. Figure 4.14 shows a handbag that has many detailed structures. However, if you were to stay far back from the bag, you would see only its basic shape and would draw it as a rectangle, as shown in the left image of Figure 4.15. By moving closer, you could see additional details such as the handles, as shown in the center image of Figure 4.15. Getting even closer, you could see many other details. All of them are actually simple, and you can handle them one level at a time.

Figure 4.14

A complicated object

Figure 4.15

A very abstract version (left), a simple version (center), and a complicated version (right)

You'll have a chance to learn more about drawing complicated objects in the next chapter. The purpose of this demonstration is to show you that every object is simple if you decide to see it as such.

Demonstrations of 2D Images

The ABC method uses the same drawing strategy for 2D images as for 3D objects. But for artists, there is still a slight difference. First, when drawing from a 2D image, you don't have to flatten it in your mind. The image is the same as the image in the picture plane if you put the image vertically in front of you. Second, the perspective theory is almost useless unless the image you want to copy is a realistic photo or painting. Otherwise, you should stick with the triangulation strategy to arrange shapes and handle structures.

When duplicating images or artwork, the human face is a favorite subject as well as the most difficult one. A person's face contains several key features: eyes, nose, mouth, ears, eyebrows, and so on. Each of these features can be considered a simple object, or at least not a complicated one. In this section, you will learn how to draw them with the ABC method.

The source image is again Van Gogh's portrait that you used for the pretest earlier in the Introduction part of this book. You probably did the pretest in a different way that time. That is perfect! You will have a chance to compare the difference between your previous effort and this one, using the new ABC method.

Eyes

Among human facial features, the eyes are the most important because they are the iconic symbol of a person. As a traditional proverb proclaims, "The eyes are the windows of the soul." We can identify the personality of a person from the eyes easier than from any other body part. In portrait drawing, if the eyes are drawn poorly, the portrait will likely end up being bad. Even though all human eyes have the same internal structures, eyes appear to have very different shapes or styles (big vs. small, smooth boundaries vs. rough edges, and so forth).

Overall, viewers are very sensitive to poorly drawn eyes. A small mistake in drawing the eyes can cause a major visual defect in a drawing. For professional artists, truly mastering drawing eyes requires a study of human facial anatomy and lots of practice.

In this demonstration, you will see that eyes can be approached with the same method as used with other objects. Basically, we treat an eye as a simple graphical structure composed of polygons. Because of the visual significance of eyes, we need to ensure a higher degree of accuracy by using more key points and reference lines in drawing eyes than almost all other objects of similar size.

The leftmost image in Figure 4.16 is the right eye of Van Gogh's portrait (seen earlier in this book's introduction). First, let's do some structural analysis to help you acquire the spatial information for that eye. Generally speaking, an eye can be represented as different basic shapes: bounding box/rectangle, oval, or polygon. I prefer using a polygon because all of its vertices are real key points that already exist in the image. If you use others—say, a bounding box—the corners of the rectangle might be virtual and thus harder to track than the real points on image.

Figure 4.16

The eye to draw (left), reference lines and key points (center left), coarsest triangulation (center right), and refinement (right)

The center-left image of Figure 4.16 shows a polygonal approximation of the outlines of the eye. In the image, 14 key points are selected from the boundaries of the eye and are denoted by hollow circles. Some reference lines are also added for support. The solid lines represent actual lines existing in the image, and the dashed lines are the virtual ones. You may find that these points and associated lines approximate the whole eye fairly well. Thus, we are going to duplicate them on paper and add some detailed refinement later.

It would be a little too complicated, however, to duplicate all 14 key points and reference lines in one step. As suggested by the ABC method, a hierarchical process needs to be applied. We simply subselect the 5 most important key points from the 14 candidates and mark them with solid circles (see the center-right image of Figure 4.16). These five points and the associated reference lines serve as a triangulation at the coarsest level. A sketch for this simple structure is completed and displayed in the leftmost image of Figure 4.17.

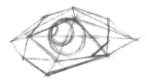

Figure 4.17

Sketch of the coarsest triangulation (left), sketch after refinement (center left), sketch before being finalized (center right), and the final drawing product (right)

For the next step, we just need to add a few more key points to refine the current triangulation. Every new point added is allocated with respect to the current triangulation. Multiple reference lines are always employed to minimize or correct errors in allocating key points. The right image of Figure 4.16 is the structure that we need to copy, and the center-left image of Figure 4.17 is the actual drawing.

Repeat this refinement by adding a few more key points. We end up with all 14 key points and a couple of circles for the pupil (see the center-right image of Figure 4.17). After some final polishing, the line drawing is done, as shown in the rightmost image of Figure 4.17.

ADAPT THE PROCESS TO YOUR SKILL LEVEL

The whole eye-drawing process seems to be lengthy because I have chopped the process into detailed baby steps for beginners so that each step is easy and has a clear goal. But this process can be adjusted to fit your skill level. As long as you feel comfortable, you can speed up this process by using larger starting triangle meshes and adding more key points at a time. Theoretically, as your skills advance, you can handle more-complicated shapes with one step, and you can finish the drawing in fewer steps. Eventually, this process becomes a standard formula, and you can quickly reach its final outcome by skipping steps. That is the ultimate goal of this training.

Nose

Drawing a nose seems to be a lot easier than drawing eyes—at least, this seems to be true for duplicating the nose displayed in the left image of Figure 4.18. However, you need be aware that a nose can be tricky at times because of the viewing angle. Symmetry and subtle detail are not easy to deal with. But we can leave this advanced topic for a future chapter.

Similar to the preceding process, we can create a series of multiresolution triangulations by starting with a very simple triangulation and then inserting more key points. The center and right images of Figure 4.18 are triangulations at two different resolutions. Figure 4.19 shows the corresponding drawing results.

Figure 4.18

Nose to draw (left), starting mesh (center), and refined mesh (right)

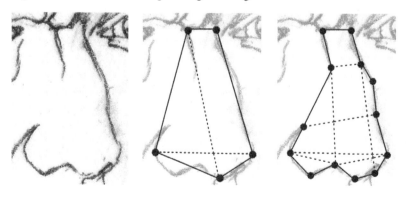

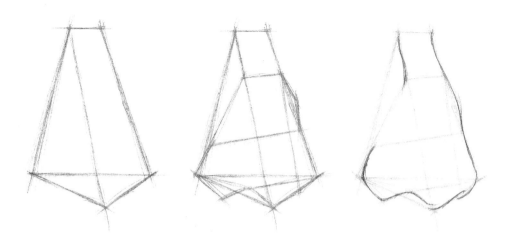

Figure 4.19

Sketch of the coarsest triangulation (left), sketch after refinement (center), and the final drawing (right)

DON'T DRAW THE NOSE TOO LONG

For some reason, beginners tend to draw long noses. This is surely a proportion issue. To avoid this mistake, you need to perform more reference checks. When you draw portraits, always shoot reference lines from the end points of the eyes to the tip of the nose. By controlling the angles of these reference lines, you will have a better chance of creating accurate proportions.

Mouth

In portrait drawing, the mouth is pretty hard to draw because it is mobile and deformable. Additionally, an open mouth includes teeth, which make the drawing much harder. Many anatomy books indicate how to draw the mouth realistically. This demonstration shows that you can treat a mouth just like any other graphical structure and process it with triangle meshes.

Figure 4.20 shows the mouth extracted from Van Gogh's portrait. As usual, a two-step triangulation is displayed. Because the mouth is typically symmetrical, we have a better selection of key points. This is just one more example demonstrating that the more we know about a target object, the more help we have in drawing it.

 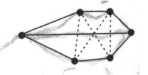 

Figure 4.20

Mouth to draw (left), starting mesh (center), and refined mesh (right)

Based on the triangulations in Figure 4.20, we can create a sequence of three images, as shown in Figure 4.21.

Figure 4.21

Sketch of the coarsest triangulation (left), sketch after refinement (center), and the final drawing (right)

Face

The last, but not least, important facial feature demonstrated here is the outline of face itself. A face is a container that holds all the facial features. The outline may range from smooth, as in a baby's face, to very bumpy, as in an old man's face. Every up-and-down in the outline is caused by muscle groups underneath the skin. Therefore, you have to make sure that the face lines match up with their underlying anatomy. Otherwise, you will find that the result of the drawing appears odd.

Again, we treat this drawing exactly the same way as before. The left image of Figure 4.22 shows the key points we can select. The resulting polygon seems to be a little bit too complicated for a single try, so we process it hierarchically in two levels. The solid circles mark the points used for the starting level, and the hollow circles represent those that were added later.

A structural copy and the final drawing are displayed in the center and right image of Figure 4.22, respectively.

Arranging all facial features inside a face is too complicated to be demonstrated at this stage. You will return to Van Gogh's face in Chapter 7 ("Using Advanced Techniques") to draw the whole face.

Figure 4.22

Key points in the face (left), a sketch duplicating the structure (center), and the final draw of the outline (right)

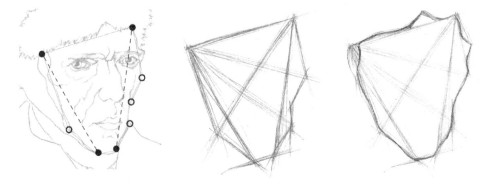

So far, you have learned how to draw simple individual objects. This is the basic skill you will need to master before trying to draw more-complicated objects in the next chapter. In the next chapter, you will draw complicated objects using the same basic method with some additional techniques to break down the complexity of objects. But before advancing to that level, please do the following exercises to strengthen your skill of drawing simple objects.

Exercises

KEY POINTS AND REFERENCE LINES

1. Find five simple objects, and do the following tasks for each of them individually:

   a. Identify 4–6 most important key points, i.e., the points that determine the most significant visual parts. Duplicate them on paper via reference lines connecting these points. Use as many reference lines as you needed.

   b. Identify more key points in the object and use the existing points you drew to allocate these new points. You may add one a time.

POLYGONS

2. Find five or more objects that have straight-line boundaries such as a laptop or a bookcase. Identify key points for each object using the method in the previous exercise. After you get these key points, selectively connect them to make polygons to represent the structures you want to draw.

OVALS

3. Draw a glass cup and focus on its oval structures (axes and proportions). Once done, put the cup in a higher or lower place and do the same exercise. Repeat this drawing for 3–5 times. Draw the object with the ABC method.

SIMPLIFICATION

4. Find five complicated objects. Draw each of them as a simple object using key points and reference lines. Draw some landscapes by using a selective drawing strategy.

2D OBJECTS

5. Find five pencil outline-drawings from the Internet. If you have hard time finding such artwork, those with light rendering should be fine too. Duplicate their lines and don't do rendering.

CHAPTER 5

Drawing Complicated Objects

A man paints with his brains and not with his hands.
—Michelangelo (1475–1564), Italian painter, sculptor, architect, and engineer

Most objects we see and draw are not as simple as a beach ball or a tissue box. Instead, these items, either natural or artificial, typically contain numerous components and small graphical features. Such detail often appears randomly, without any regular pattern. Being able to draw these complex objects is the next level you need to achieve, and this chapter is going to guide your advancement toward this goal.

The amount of graphical information to extract and process from a complicated object is usually far more than that from a simple one. Obviously, this structural complexity results in a high degree of drawing difficulty. When we lay out a large number of graphics on paper, one spatial mistake can trigger many other issues—with catastrophic results. Therefore, a scientific solution is required more than ever. You need to acquire some techniques that teach you how to deal with pictorial information in a systematic manner. Otherwise, moving to the next level simply through practice will take you a long time.

In this chapter, you will learn the following techniques as you follow along with demonstrations:

- **Breaking down complexity**
- **Using virtual structures**

Breaking Down Complexity

It is difficult to create a good-quality drawing of a complicated object without breaking it down to simple components and sketching them first. There are two major strategies to breaking down the drawing complexity. One is to simplify objects, and the other is to re-organize objects' structures in multiple layers so that each layer contains simple structures. The former mainly focuses on single-level graphical structures, while the latter works on multiple levels. Both strategies are independent, so they can work together; as you will see, most of the time we use a mixture of both.

Simplifying objects is not a new strategy. Artists have used this approach for a long time. A popular method is approximating complicated components with ovals or rectangles for overall planning as well as for filtering out unwanted noises. This tactic fits the principle of divide and conquer. But current art books rarely mention how to put these simplified shapes together to form an overall solution. This missing piece is actually a core part of the drawing process. Without a systematic approach, the traditional methods appear inadequate and inefficient. Moreover, it is hard for beginners to pick up such an approach without fully understanding why and how it works.

Re-organizing a complicated object in multiple simple layers is another way to make drawing easier to implement. Because many complicated objects are structured hierarchically, artists in the past took this approach to a certain degree. However, lacking a solid theory to guide such practices, this approach was not fully explored and utilized.

In this section, you will learn several techniques that break a complicated object down to a level that enables you to draw it with ease. Most of them are combination of simplification and re-organizing strategies. They all work well with the ABC method. These tactics are the vehicles you will use to bring your drawing skill to the next level, by sharpening your ability to handle various graphical structures scientifically.

Ignoring Detail

Every object has graphical details at various levels, from a big framework to tiny micro-features. The complexity of a structure depends how much we see or want to draw. There is a simple and commonly used strategy to simplify objects: nonstraight lines are made to be straight, rounded curves are replaced by circles or ovals, and a highly detailed polygon is approximated with a simpler polygon. The basic principle is to ignore small features or filter out unwanted nuances. Using this approach, a little complicated object can be drawn as a simple one. Chapter 4, "Drawing Simple Objects," already addressed this concept.

Using Boolean Operations

Boolean operations are mathematical processes that are used to break a complicated object into several simple ones. Technically, any object can be presented and created with a sequence of Boolean operations. Union, one of the three Boolean operations, allows us to merge two sets to form a new one. In art, we can use the operation in reverse order to separate an object into two simpler pieces. Many artists use this natural and intuitive strategy to separate graphical components and reduce drawing complexity.

When we use the union operation to split objects, it's like using the difference Boolean operation, which is the same as addition or subtraction in mathematics. The Boolean intersection operation is rarely used in drawing, but one of its applications, shape overlapping, will be introduced in the next chapter.

Disassembling man-made machinery into simpler components is fairly straightforward, for instance. Engineers often design complicated devices by integrating simple, movable forms so that each part is easy to add or remove for effective manufacturing and assembling. For example, a table consists of a top face and a few legs; a computer keyboard has a rectangular-shaped base attached to many small cubes (the keys). Obviously, we can view this kind of object as a union of small parts and then conquer each component individually. Isolating components enables us to quickly reduce drawing complexity.

The left image of Figure 5.1 shows a spray bottle that has a body, a neck, and a nozzle. Because each component is easy to identify and separate, we can then divide the object visually into three parts. Each one is bounded by a rectangle or other quadrilateral (see the center image of Figure 5.1). This treatment quickly turns the drawing task into three subtasks that are simple enough to handle individually.

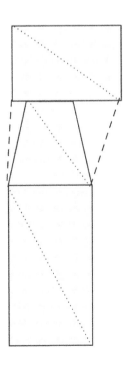

Figure 5.1

Spray bottle (left), with bounding rectangles and quadrilaterals (center), and decomposition (right)

Disassembling the subject is only half of the drawing process. The other half—a more important and a more difficult step—is to draw each part with the correct relationships and proportions in order to rebuild the entire object. This process requires us to produce the overall arrangement, and this should be done before we sketch out the detailed components. Therefore, we need to use reference lines to acquire spatial information about these bounding polygons. In the right image of Figure 5.1, diagonal lines are shown as dotted lines to manage proportions; reference lines, denoted by dashed lines, are set up to align the bounding boxes.

In Figure 5.1, we see that the three polygons are stacked on top of each other without rotations. These spatial properties help us to reduce DOFs so that the main task of obtaining structural information is controlling the proportions of the bounding polygons.

Figure 5.2 shows the process of planning and drawing the separated parts for the sprayer. First we sketch the bounding polygons and confirm their relationships with reference lines. Because we treat each part as an isolated, simple object, we don't need to worry about the structure inside a bounding polygon until the overall arrangement is complete. In the next step, you should be able to use the techniques covered in the preceding chapter to draw each part individually. The center image of Figure 5.2 is the sketch of the detailed construction, and the right image is the final drawing.

Figure 5.2

Bounding polygons (left), detail added (center), and final drawing (right)

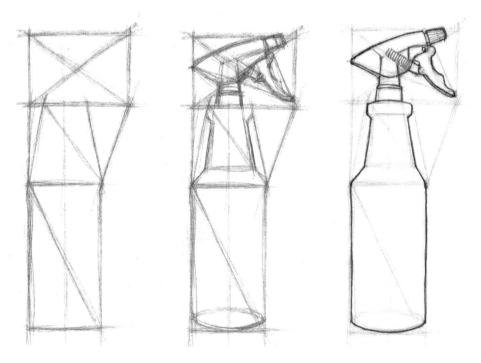

Creating Hierarchical Structures

It is not always easy to disassemble a complicated object into clearly defined pieces. In certain cases, components might mix together or overlap with each other so that they are hard to separate. Natural objects typically have this property. For example, a rose has many petals, and each petal is a simple object. But the petals stick together and form a very tight structure. Disassembling such an object anatomically does not bring us much benefit—actually, it complicates things.

Figure 5.3 shows one example in which each flower petal is separated from the flower body with a rectangle. The left image is the object, and the right image displays bounding boxes covering some of the petals. The large number of overlapping box shapes doesn't simplify the image at all. Instead, the busy rectangles in the scene might frustrate inexperienced artists.

 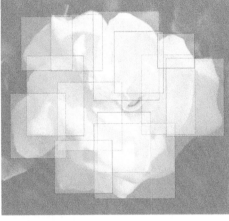

Figure 5.3

Rose (left) and bounding boxes of some petals (right)

The reason that the separating strategy does not work well in this example is that the rose contains too many static graphical structures (petals). Accessing each individual structure simultaneously is too complicated for most of us. Additionally, the overlapping rectangles result in many irregular shapes. In this case, approaching the dynamic graphical structures hierarchically is a better solution. In other words, we can identify shapes based on visual patterns and arrange them in multiple resolutions. The irregularly formatted petals form many regular dynamic shapes of different sizes. These shapes provide a simple but powerful way for us to restore the entire flower, by duplicating these multiresolution shapes layer by layer.

That being said, we need to represent the entire image as a sequence of graphical structures. Each step in the sequence involves a simple process. The first three images of Figure 5.4 show the creation of a hierarchical structure by using triangulation. Starting with a few key points, we represent the rose as a quadrilateral, or a triangulation with only two triangles. After we lay out these four points, we use them to allocate a few additional key points. The third image shows the vertex set, in which the newly added points are represented by smaller black dots. The reference lines connecting key points are then used to allocate new points.

Keep in mind that the most important thing here is to allocate new key points, not to build triangles. Triangulation and the associated lines are used only to help us pinpoint the key points. Because the key points are used as landmarks in the image, the more we have, the more structural information we will have on paper. After we construct enough key points, we are then able to draw detailed features based on those key points. The right image of Figure 5.4 is that drawing.

The beauty of this hierarchical approach is that it helps you organize graphical information in different layers based on their visual priority. At each layer, you need to increase only a small number of structures. After you have done this, you can repeat the process and move on to the next step. Therefore, the complexity of the drawing is greatly reduced to a comfortable level, where you can complete the job without much difficulty.

Figure 5.4

Starting mesh (top left), refinement (top right), one more refinement (bottom left), and final drawing (bottom right)

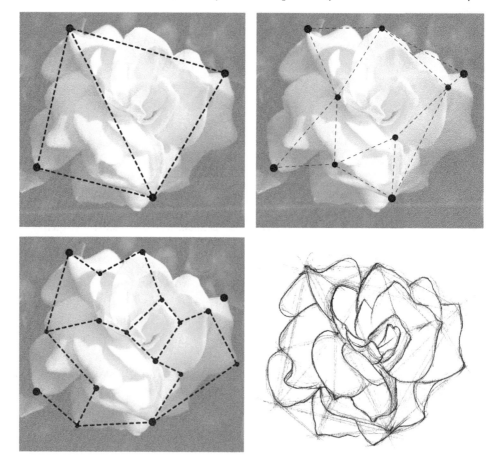

Using Virtual Skeletons

The multiresolution triangulation solution, which originated from CG, is a general-purpose method designed to solve structure problems associated with complicated objects. The triangles at different scales allow us to process graphical information progressively. The edges of the triangles, or the lines between triangle vertices, serve as a network across an image and hold all graphical details together efficiently. In Chapter 4, these edges are said to form the *virtual skeleton* of the object that has no natural skeletal structure.

If an object has a natural skeleton, we must take maximum advantage of such important information. Obviously, the human body is the best example of this. Because of the importance of figure drawing, I dedicate all of Chapter 8, "Using Special Techniques for Drawing Human Bodies," to this topic. Thus, I do not address the human skeleton here.

Trees are another representative form that has skeletal structures. A tree has a trunk and several branches attached to that trunk. Each branch then has multiple smaller branches extending from it, and this pattern keeps going until we reach the leaves. The tree configuration can be easily seen as an anatomical system in which each branch acts as a bone. This process allows us to describe and construct a tree easily and precisely. It has been used in CG software to create realistic plants.

Fractals are another example showing that understanding the anatomical structure behind objects can dramatically simplify the drawing process. Koch curves (shown earlier in Chapter 2, "Extracting Graphical Structures—A Scientific Point of View") are ultra-complicated curves created by a simple rule. If we don't know the rule behind the structure, creating such fractal objects becomes extremely hard. Fractal theory, a branch of mathematics born in the 1980s, has radically changed the way we look at complicated objects. Fractal theory demystifies the hidden patterns of many natural objects such as plants, clouds, rivers, and terrains. Contrary to public perception, these objects have very simple structures despite the complexity of their appearance. For artists, fractal analysis has resulted in a new way of creating complicated objects.

Figure 5.5 shows the abstract skeleton pattern in a general tree structure. The fractal constructive process starts with a single line segment as the trunk and then grows a few branches in different directions and at different sizes. These two steps make up a basic tree growth pattern. Only three steps are displayed in Figure 5.5, but obviously the pattern can be applied to any new branch and can keep the abstract tree growing.

By using curved lines and by varying branch sizes, angles, and total numbers at every step, we can turn the abstract tree skeleton into a realistic tree. Figure 5.6 shows a simple example of such a procedure.

Figure 5.5

An abstract tree structure

Figure 5.6

**A realistic tree draw-
ing using a fractal
concept**

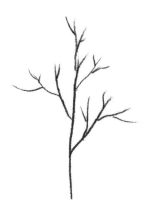

The parts of an average still object, particularly if those parts are thin and lengthy, can be viewed and treated as "bones" of that object. Many objects have such virtual skeletons, which are easy to identify: flowers, table lamps, a tripod, and so forth. To extract the information, you can simply replace a thin part as a line segment for quick and efficient processing. Figure 5.7 demonstrates two examples in which sticks replace components.

Using virtual skeletons enables us to quickly identify important key points. These points are landmarks or joints in the skeleton configurations. Sometimes these points are not visually noticeable or are even completely invisible, such as joints in clothed human figures. But an understanding of object structures can always help us find hidden information useful in planning structures on paper.

Figure 5.7

**Skeleton in a flower
(left) and skeleton in
a tripod (right)**

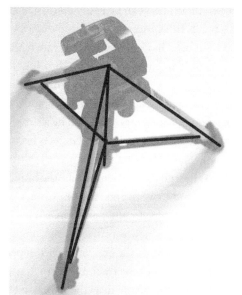

Discovering Hidden Patterns

Some complicated objects have their components arranged in certain geometric configurations, such as lines or circles. This is particularly true for industrial products in which small parts are often oriented uniformly and regularly. For example, keys on a telephone pad are organized in a grid, the slats of mini blinds are grouped in parallel, the numbers on the face of a clock appear in a circle, and so on. After you discover such simple patterns, the task of laying out graphical structures on paper becomes much easier. You can efficiently arrange all of these parts together by using the designed pattern rather than handling each one individually.

Remember, when you see highly detailed objects, always try to take a closer look to see whether any special pattern exists within them. These features are a free gift that can help you complete a drawing more efficiently. Figure 5.8 shows several patterns in various objects.

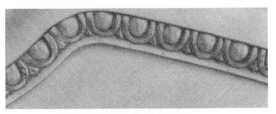

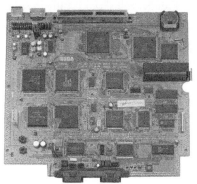

Figure 5.8

Repeated decorative feature on furniture (top left), circle format in the Space Needle (right), and lots of geometric patterns on a computer motherboard (bottom left)

SOURCE: http://en.wikipedia.org/wiki/File:Sega-Saturn-Motherboard.jpg

Drawing Selectively and Symbolically

Creating an observational drawing does not mean you that have to put everything you see on paper. That is neither feasible nor necessary. An object always contains various kinds of visual information that might not be important or interesting. One such feature is the texture of materials. Walls, carpets, clothes, and human skin all have tiny, but visible, graphical patterns. This kind of textural information is used for decoration and has little use in the configuration of the object. Therefore, it is a common practice to ignore such textures or simply pretend not to see them.

One tricky issue is handling details that *have* structural value. Winkles in clothes, tree leaves, and human hair are some examples you see every day. What should we do with them? Deciding whether to select or ignore a structural detail is really a matter of personal preference. There is probably no scientific way to evaluate the importance of such details. You can simply choose to ignore some of these structures to make your job easier. If you decide to keep them, you can still reduce complexity by drawing them symbolically. For instance, after you sketch the big structures of a tree, you can add some leaves at a selected area, and these leaves don't need to be an exact copy of the real ones. You can use the same strategy to handle drawing hair. While duplicating the overall shapes you observed, the detailed part can be accomplished by drawing some strands symbolically to represent a more massive amount of hair. Figure 5.9 demonstrates an example.

Figure 5.9
Selective drawing
of hair

The techniques addressed in this section are all general-purpose approaches for making sketching complicated objects easier. If you want to get further help for drawing a particular object such as an animal or automobile, you should study the object to extract and duplicate its unique graphical structures. While using left-brain processing, you will gain a deep understanding of the patterns in the object by studying it in depth.

Demonstrations

Generally speaking, before starting to draw, you always need to take a look at the subject and see whether there is any unique structural information that can help you with your drawing. If the object is too complicated, you need to divide it into smaller pieces and/or arrange graphical information in different layers.

In this section, you will see demonstrations of drawing various complicated objects. The techniques presented earlier will be used to process graphical structures. Using these techniques, you will find that drawing complicated objects can be greatly simplified and therefore easy to learn. After following along with the structural analysis and step-by-step drawing procedures, you should reread each demonstration and practice the drawing techniques you've learned so far in this book. Be aware that each demonstration illustrates just one way to execute the techniques, and that may not be the best way. Feel free to try different ways to pick key points, references, and shapes other than the ones used in the demonstrations.

Lightbulb

The lightbulb shown in the left image of Figure 5.10 obviously has three separate parts. On top, it has a thin, spiral pipeline that is in the general shape of a cylinder. The center and bottom parts are both simple cylinders. Additionally, the object is symmetrical along a centerline. From these observations, this not-too-complicated object can be divided into three parts, as indicated by the highlighted quadrilateral regions in the center image of

Figure 5.10. The corners of these three areas, marked by black dots, are the key points we want to allocate. The dashed lines are references that we are going to use to align these points on paper.

The left image of Figure 5.11 is the outline of the three parts. Make sure to draw these lines very lightly because they are just supporting lines that are not needed in the final artwork.

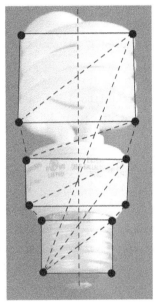

Figure 5.10

Lightbulb (left), partitioning (center), and further analysis of the top part (right)

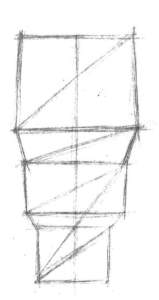

Figure 5.11

Outline of the three parts of the lightbulb (left), sketch of all the structures (center), and final drawing (right)

After the separation, only the top part is too complicated to duplicate in one step, while the other two parts are simple enough for you to duplicate. The right image of Figure 5.10 shows further analysis of the top part. Because of its spiral structure, this part is represented by three tilted ovals that partially overlap in a parallel manner. Arranging them within the quadrilateral region allows you to have a sketch of all the structures (see the center image of Figure 5.11). At this moment, none of the sketch lines is finalized yet. There is still a chance to check the drawing and correct mistakes before committing to drawing heavy, clean lines. The right image of Figure 5.11 is the final result.

There is one tricky issue with this demonstration. You may have noticed that I did not use a bounding box to approximate the three parts. Instead, I used quadrilaterals that do not even cover the entire regions of interest. I did this for visual convenience. If a rounded region is approximated by a bounding box, as shown in Figure 5.12, all four corner points will not be on the actual object. Using these virtual points as a visual reference then becomes difficult. You will learn about advanced approaches for this challenge in Chapter 7 ("Using Advanced Techniques"). For now, I suggest that beginners use the simple approach described here.

Figure 5.12

Avoid using non-existing corner points.

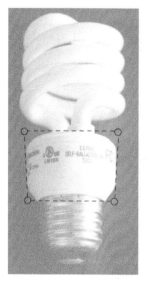

Fabric

Fabric is a pretty popular object in drawing. When you draw people, you cannot avoid drawing clothes consisting of different materials. Unlike most other objects, fabric is dynamic and has wrinkles and decorations. In this demonstration, you will learn how to draw a portion of a school backpack that has many small parts (see the left image of Figure 5.13).

Figure 5.13

A piece of fabric (left), partitioning (center), and further structural analysis (right)

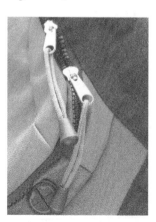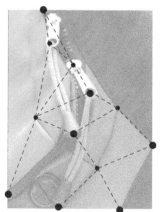

The targeted region has dynamic structures without any regular patterns. Therefore, we need to find a small number of key points to divide the image into small zones. The center image of Figure 5.13 shows the points selected for an initial subdivision. Each solid line connecting two key points indicates that these points have an actual connection in the object. Dashed lines are imaginary. But both solid and dashed lines are used as references to selected key points. The left image of Figure 5.14 is an actual sketch of these key points and the corresponding reference lines.

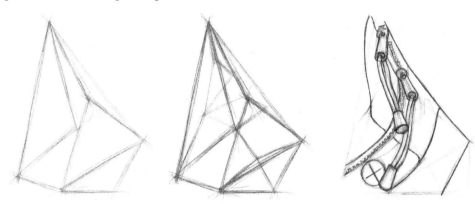

Figure 5.14

Outline of initial partitioning (left), more key points added (center), and final drawing (right)

With this primary partitioning done, a few more key points are selected. In the right image of Figure 5.13, the smaller black dots represent the newly added points, and the larger dots are already allocated. To select these newly added points on paper, we have to use all the previously established key points. The dashed lines provide the various ready-to-use references you'll need to complete this task. The center image of Figure 5.14 is the drawing of this step.

After we have all of the key points on paper, adding all the details becomes straightforward. The right image of Figure 5.14 shows the finished drawing.

DRAWING FABRIC

It may seem like overkill to allocate key points so precisely just to draw fabric. In reality, drawing fabric can be a much looser and faster process, because most people won't even know whether the wrinkles are accurate. This demonstration is designed to show you how the ABC method works for dynamic structures like fabrics. If a future drawing task does not require a high degree of accuracy, you can use fewer key points and steps to establish the structures.

Shoe

A shoe is hard to draw, not just because of its structure but also because of its curved shapes. This demonstration shows how to draw a woman's shoe. For simplicity, we will draw a side view, but a more complicated example is demonstrated in Chapter 6 ("Drawing Complicated Scenes").

The left image of Figure 5.15 shows a typical shoe. It looks like a big triangular shape, but we know that a quadrilateral is a better choice for an initial approximation because we can find all vertices on the boundaries of the shoe. The center image of Figure 5.15 shows a few key points picked from the shoe and the associated connections between these points.

Figure 5.15

A shoe (left), partitioning (center), and further structural analysis (right)

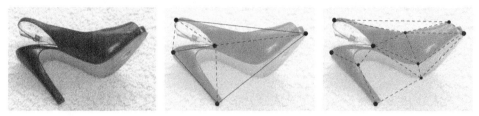

The structure of the shoe is very prone to errors. A minor mistake can make the shoe look bad because we are so familiar with the curves on shoes. Thus, we need to employ more key points to achieve sufficient accuracy. Based on our general understanding of shoes, it is pretty easy to identify the next round of key points (see the right image of Figure 5.15).

Figure 5.16 is a series of images of the actual drawing based on the analysis shown in Figure 5.15. We start by sketching a simple quadrilateral. We then add more points based on the preceding step. The resulting triangulation makes this process seem complicated. However, the reality is that you add key points one at a time, using reference lines from any existing point, so this progressive approach is accomplished in small, doable steps. After you lay out all structures lightly on paper, make sure that the sketch looks okay before finalizing all the lines (see the right image of Figure 5.16).

Figure 5.16

Initial partitioning (top left), more key points allocated (top right), sketch of all the structures (bottom right), and the final drawing (bottom left)

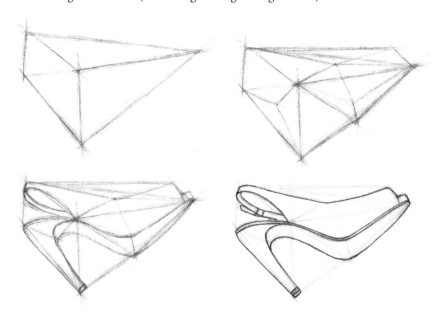

Lamp

The next demonstration shows how to draw an old table lamp that has many detailed features. In this example, you will learn how to handle complicated structures selectively.

First, let's do a quick structural analysis: the lamp (the left image of Figure 5.17) is quite symmetrical with respect to a centerline. It has two separate parts—a shade that is a simple cone or trapezoid shape and a more complicated body. Based on this simple fact, the lamp is separated into two parts by six key points (see the center-left image of Figure 5.17). These points control the overall proportions of the lamp.

The left image of Figure 5.18 shows the duplication of the key points and the triangulation generated. Make sure to put in a centerline because it is an important aid to drawing.

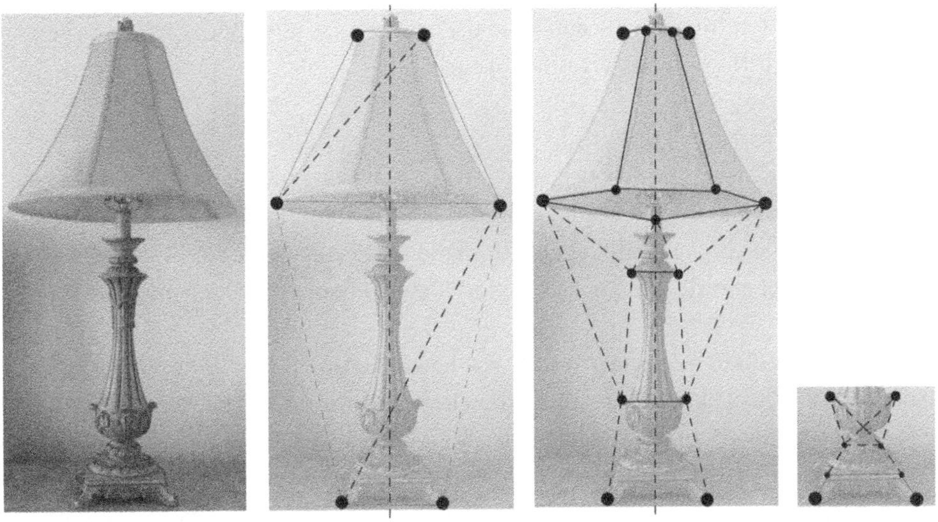

Figure 5.17

A lamp (left), initial partitioning (center left), further refinement (center right), and local refinement of the base (right)

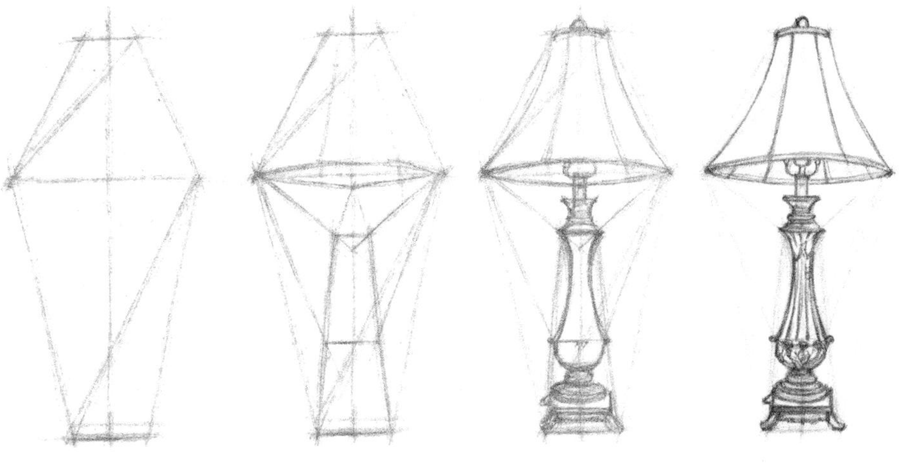

Figure 5.18

Initial partitioning (left), more key points allocated (center left), sketch of all the structures (center right), and the final drawing (right)

Further refinement is the next step, particularly in the lamp base, where more graphical structures need to be extracted. The center-right image of Figure 5.17 displays the newly added key points and their relationships to the previous key points. These points are selected according to their visual importance to help us control detailed features. The center-left image of Figure 5.18 is the corresponding drawing.

The image is controlled with many key points. You can start to add detailed features at this point. If you find that the base area still needs more key points because of its greater detail, you can add a few in that area, as indicated by the right image of Figure 5.17.

The center-right image of Figure 5.18 is the sketch of big structures based on the information acquired so far. If you stop at this level, it is still a fairly good drawing with enough features expressed. But the visual patterns in the middle area are so appealing that you might like to have some of them in the final version. Additionally, these decorations make an interesting visual contrast to the lamp shade—the upper part has large blank areas, while the bottom part is full of curves.

Hand

You have probably heard from artists that drawing hands is extremely difficult. A hand consists of a palm and five fingers. Each finger has a few joints that allow the finger to bend and flex. Such high mobility makes the hand a super-dynamic object that is able to form hundreds of gestures. You may even find some art books that teach only the drawing of hands.

Figure 5.19

A V sign (left), initial partitioning (center left), adding key points for the other three fingers (center right), and controlling the details of fingers (right)

This demonstration is designed to show you how the triangulation principle can be used to deal with a human hand. The gesture to duplicate is a victory (V) sign (see the left image of Figure 5.19). Obviously, you can immediately decompose this image into two parts: the palm and the two extended fingers. The two fingers can be processed together as a quadrilateral, so we need four key points to identify the shape. The center-left image of Figure 5.19 is the initial partitioning of the hand. At the moment, you don't need to worry about the other three fingers because they are contained in the shape that represents the palm.

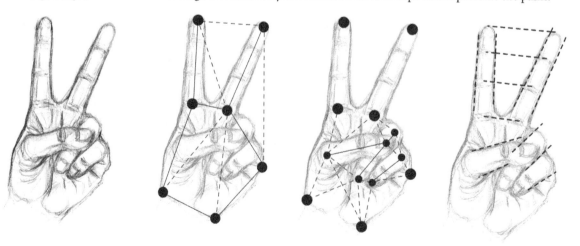

The next step is to control the other three fingers by adding some key points. Because all fingers are generally long and thin, it is natural to select a finger's end points as key points. The center-right image of Figure 5.19 is the result of adding a few more key points. They are all inside the palm area, and the previously established key points are used to allocate these new points. So far, we have used a single line to represent each finger. This line indicates the length of a finger, but information about the width is missing. To indicate the thickness of each finger, you need to add a few parallel reference lines, as shown in the right image of Figure 5.19. Reference lines are also used to partition the two stretched fingers for the locations of joints.

The first two images of Figure 5.20 show the drawing process of laying out the key points and the triangulation/polygons on paper. At this point, the orientation of each finger is represented by a single line. Finger width and joint length are the detailed information that still needs to be acquired. After we have set up all the major structures inside the hand, detailed lines can be finalized to complete the work. The last two images of Figure 5.20 show these steps.

Figure 5.20

Initial partitioning (left), key points for the other three fingers (center left), sketching all fingers (center right), and the final drawing (right)

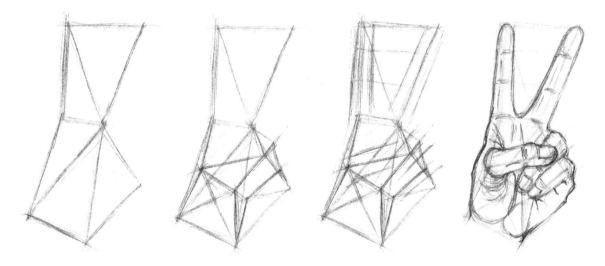

PRACTICE

Hands are very hard to draw, especially for beginners. The good news is that you'll have plenty of opportunity to practice. You'll just need a pencil and paper and then draw your own hands! You can make a gesture with one hand and then draw it with the other hand. So if you have time but don't know what to draw, think about drawing your hands.

Tripod

Foreshortening happens when you view a long object along its axis. In this case, the long object will appear compressed. This phenomenon is pretty common in figure drawings when a model's arms, legs, or torso are oriented toward you. Foreshortening is one of the most difficult things to portray in observational drawing. Beginners often have trouble deciding the lengths of foreshortened components. In this section, you will learn how to use triangulation to solve this problem efficiently.

Because of the complexity of human figures, this demonstration uses a tripod to teach you about foreshortening. In this case, you will duplicate a foreshortened tripod, as shown in the left image of Figure 5.21. The object has three equal-length legs, but they look quite different from one another because of the top-down view. It is easy to see that the three legs are still the major structures in the object, and they deserve immediate action to establish them. The center image of Figure 5.21 shows the key points representing the legs. The resulting graphical structure is a quadrilateral that represents a pretty good starting point.

Figure 5.21

A tripod (left), key points for the three legs (center), and refinement for the rest of the major structures (right)

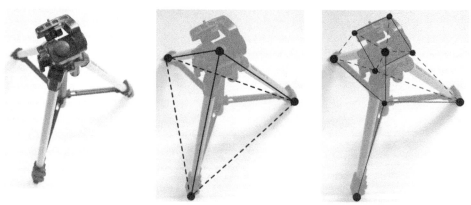

As you lay out the three legs on paper, double-check their lengths by using the available reference lines. The left image of Figure 5.22 displays the drawing of this step.

After the three legs are under control, adding key points for the rest of the structures is fairly easy. There are a few small structures on the top of the tripod, and these structures together form a little distorted rectangle. Using the previous key points, however, should be enough to lock the positions of the four corners of the rectangle.

The second image of Figure 5.22 is the sketch of these points. The rectangle contains many other tiny parts. However, we don't have to use key points for them, because they are all simple shapes. We can draw these unimportant graphical structures directly. The last two images in Figure 5.22 show the arrangement of all structures and the finalized drawing.

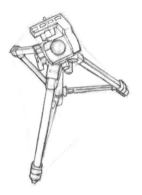

Figure 5.22

Duplicating the key points of the three legs (left), adding more key points and reference lines (center left), sketching all the major structures (center right), and the final drawing (right)

Trees and Plants

Trees and plants are essential parts of landscape drawing. Unlike the objects we have drawn so far, a tree has a lot of detail, and using triangulation to create all visible structures would be absolutely impossible (and unnecessary). That does not mean that you don't need to manage a tree's overall shape when you draw the tree. This demonstration is designed to show you how the ABC method can be applied to drawing a giant bird-of-paradise plant, which is popular in the southern United States.

The left image of Figure 5.23 is the subject we want to draw. Obviously, the plant contains a large number of interesting structures. We will not duplicate every one of them or spend much time duplicating each structure precisely. Instead, we will set up a simple structural framework for quick control of the object (see the right image of Figure 5.23). This framework consists of only a few lines that act as a skeleton to support the whole plant. Various structures can be quickly added with reasonable accuracy. The left image of Figure 5.24 is a loose sketch of the structures.

Figure 5.23

A giant bird-of-paradise (left) and its simple framework (right)

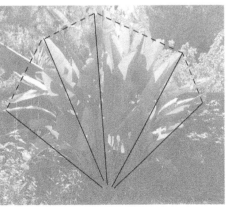

Figure 5.24
**Loose sketch of the
structures (left) and
selectively drawn
detail (right)**

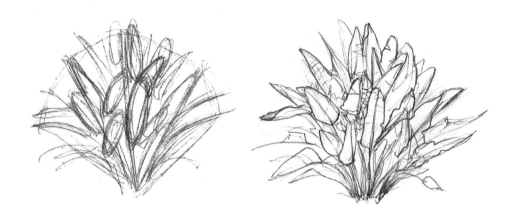

To finish the drawing, you don't have to draw every single piece of the plant. Instead, select a piece that you like or that is visually important. The rest can be either ignored or replaced by some random leaf-patterns.

Lego Toy

A favorite subject of perspective drawing is an object with many parallel lines. In the ABC method, we don't use vanishing points or the horizon line for aligning objects. In this demonstration, you will learn how to draw a Lego toy that has many parallel lines in 3D space.

Figure 5.25
**Lego toy (left), key
points for the major
body (center left),
key points for cylin-
ders (center right),
and ovals to extract
(right)**

Generally speaking, all parallel 3D lines "bend," according to the perspective theory. How much they bend depends on the object's distance vs. its size. In this demonstration, the object is pretty small (see the left image of Figure 5.25). So even if the object is viewed closely, the parallel lines do not distort much. You can start with a simple version—drawing without an orthogonal view and then adding some correction to compensate for the small distortion.

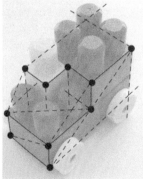

The center-left image of Figure 5.25 is the collection of key points that are used to represent the major body. At this moment, you should ignore all the cylinders, including the wheels. There are too many to conquer at this point. We need to do one thing a time and approach the complicated image in a step-by-step manner.

The left image of Figure 5.26 is the sketch on paper for the main body. You can see that it consists of several standard cubes. There are many parallel lines in this image.

The next step is to add small cylinders. Clearly, each of these cylinders is primarily controlled by the center point of its top face. Therefore, these center points are selected as the next round of key points. Because these cylinders have a obvious parallel configuration, the center points are aligned in parallel. You can see this in the center-right image of Figure 5.25 as well as in the center-left image of Figure 5.26.

Figure 5.26

Draw the main body part with a few key points (left), add key points to control cylinders (center left), and sketch all cylinders (center right). The final drawing (right).

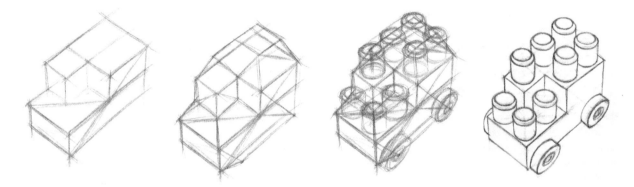

The last pieces of structural information that still need to be extracted are the ovals. To draw an oval correctly, you first need to determine its two axes. In this example, every oval is the perspective view of a circle on the top surface of a cylinder; therefore, the minor axis of each oval is parallel to the centerline of the cylinder. In the right image of Figure 5.25, three ovals are displayed together with their axes. An arrow near an oval represents the centerline direction of the cylinder for that oval. Because of the perspective view, the centerline directions are a bit distorted. We will add them back into the drawing later.

The ovals' proportions are also important. In this demonstration, however, you don't have to do extra work because the cubes beneath the cylinders already tell us how a square is deformed. This is enough information to decide the proportions of the ovals, and you can sketch them directly on the top of the structures completed thus far. The center-right image of Figure 5.26 shows all the loosely drawn cylinders. The rightmost image of Figure 5.26 is the final drawing with some correction to give the cylinders a less-than-parallel appearance.

Exercises

DECONSTRUCTION WITH BOOLEAN OPERATIONS

1. Find five complicated objects, and do the following tasks for each of them individually:

    a. Identify substructures and draw them with bounding boxes only.

    b. Identify substructures and draw them with bounding polygons.

VIRTUAL SKELETONS

2. Find an object that has multiple large, thin components. Use two to three key points to represent each component, and then connect these key points to construct a skeleton for the entire object. If you have trouble finding an object, consider different types of animals or insects.

PERSPECTIVE VIEW

3. Place a complicated object very close to you, and orient the object so that some noticeable foreshortening is present. Draw the object with the ABC method.

    Note: If you are familiar with perspective drawing, do not create vanishing points here. This exercise will prove that you can draw objects very realistically without using the perspective drawing method.

KEY POINTS AND REFERENCE LINES

4. Find five complicated objects. For each of them, identify some key points and draw reference lines on paper.

    a. In this exercise, no details need to be drawn because the focus is to identify key points.

    b. Try to find some key points that have extra spatial relationships, such as two points that are aligned vertically or horizontally, three or more points that are on the same line, points forming a square or an equilateral triangle, and so forth.

5. Draw the toy dinosaur shown in Figure 5.27 by using all techniques you've learned thus far. Find another four complicated objects to draw in similar way.

6. Draw some landscapes by using a selective drawing strategy.

Figure 5.27
Toy dinosaur

CHAPTER 6

Drawing Complicated Scenes

The whole is simpler than the sum of its parts.

— JOSIAH WILLARD GIBBS (1839–1903), AMERICAN THEORETICAL PHYSICIST,

CHEMIST, AND MATHEMATICIAN

So far, you have learned various techniques for processing individual objects. The ability to handle items independently is a fundamental drawing skill. But artwork rarely contains a single object. Artists typically put multiple objects with different materials and shapes together to achieve visual harmony. Because there is no natural bond between such objects, you can organize them in any way you want for an observational drawing. However, this doesn't mean you can draw them randomly on paper. After a scene is set, you need to duplicate not only individual objects but also the spatial relationships between them. Therefore, it is essential to acquire the skill of managing multiple objects efficiently.

Obviously, all the techniques you have used to draw objects individually still apply. But you still need some additional strategies to handle the spatial relationships among different objects in a complicated scene.

This chapter presents demonstrations of these strategies. You will learn how to use the following techniques:

- Creating big graphical structures by grouping graphical structures
- Merging objects with overlapping shapes
- Organizing a group of objects via virtual skeletons
- Adjusting the small structures by using negative space

Introducing Techniques for Merging Objects

You may notice that drawing multiple objects is similar to drawing components of a complicated object. The former deals with separate objects that may or may not have any association, while the latter is processing parts that are naturally bonded. Surely, these two cases share an important feature: a large number of graphical structures or a high degree of complexity.

The difference is the relationship between graphical structures. When an object contains many parts, you can view and process them independently. But the natural bonds or hidden connections among these components allow you to handle the spatial relationship much faster and more accurately. In Chapter 5, "Drawing Complicated Objects," you learned how petals on a rose, legs on a tripod, and fingers on a hand are processed together. The obvious linkage among the components of an object provides extremely useful tips for managing structures. However, sometimes such connections are hidden and are not easy to find. For example, an inexperienced artist may feel that the eyes, nose, mouth, and ear are completely independent because they are separate components on a head. This easily results in incorrect proportions and positions of these structures. Artists who are familiar with human anatomy, however, will use the structural relationships among these facial features to draw a face correctly on paper.

When you draw a scene with a group of random objects, there are no natural or static connections among these items. This feature *seems* to make drawing easier, because people can overlook the errors in your work. For example, if you draw two apples closer than they actually are on a table, no one will likely notice. But if you want to draw the entire scene perfectly, your task will be much harder. In this case, you don't have any obvious patterns to help you align different items. For instance, there is no logical or natural association between an apple and a cup on a table.

Sometimes the boundary between a complicated object and a scene of multiple objects is not clear. You can view a setting as one single complex object or as a group of unrelated items. For instance, you may consider automobiles in a parking lot as independent objects, but you can also view them in a special format defined by their parking spots. The flowers of a plant surely are parts of the same object, but they can be viewed as individual unrelated items because their spatial relationship is so weak.

In the ABC method, we treat both cases in fairly similar ways. We want to maximize the use of any obvious structural patterns to assist in our drawing. More important, we want to discover some hidden patterns or create some virtual patterns by linking various structures in a way that favors or supports our drawing. Although different items may not have a natural bond, as long as they are put into the same scene, their graphical structures are automatically connected by their spatial relationship. In other words, everything we draw on paper should somehow be considered connected. The traditional negative-space technique is an attempt to connect separate objects with the blank space (negative space) between them. However, such a strategy does not give us much help for arranging big, complex scenes quickly on paper. Similar to simplifying a complicated object, we solve this problem by integrating items to *create* bigger structures.

That being said, the ABC method processes multiple objects by merging them "intelligently" in order to achieve some useful patterns. In this section, you will learn several techniques for discovering such patterns and using them to organize graphical structures for a better, finished drawing.

Grouping Graphical Structures

An item in a complicated scene may or may not have a natural connection with the rest of the scene. Even if there is a hidden association, you might not have time to figure that out in your drawing. Certainly, we cannot do much about it, because most of the time we either don't have the knowledge (such as with anatomy) or we don't have the right viewing position. For instance, you might not be able to see the spatial pattern between your house and your neighbor's house until you get a bird's-eye view of both houses together or see it from a satellite image. The good news is that you don't have to find such *static* structures in order to draw accurately. An alternative, but efficient, solution is using grouped graphical structures that already exist in the scene.

In Chapter 2, "Extracting Graphical Structures—A Scientific Point of View," you learned that a grouped GS is a kind of dynamic GS formed by independent objects, based on your viewing position. When multiple objects are placed in a scene, you can always find many useful spatial patterns that connect unrelated points. This kind of GS is very valuable for arranging and drawing shapes on paper.

The top-left image of Figure 6.1 shows a picture of many pens that are randomly positioned on a table. Although each pen can easily be drawn as a thin rectangle, duplicating all of the pens with the correct locations and orientations is a challenging task.

Obviously, these pens are independent objects, and there is no predesigned pattern for their arrangement. We have to use some sophisticated strategies to acquire the spatial information and help us to plan these shapes on paper. A grouped GS works very well for solving these kinds of problems.

The center and right images in the top row of Figure 6.1 highlight a few big grouped GSs in the scene. For your convenience, they are displayed in separate images. These GSs have simple shapes that are easy to duplicate. After we make a copy of these polygonal shapes on paper, the whole scene is partitioned by the polygons (see the left image in the bottom row of Figure 6.1). Therefore, it is straightforward to add individual pens in the subdivided regions and to accomplish the job as shown by the other two images in the bottom row.

This way to merge objects is not unique. You can group items in different combinations based on your observation and understanding of the scene. To make drawing efficient, you should always find large and simple groupings of objects to help your overall layout first.

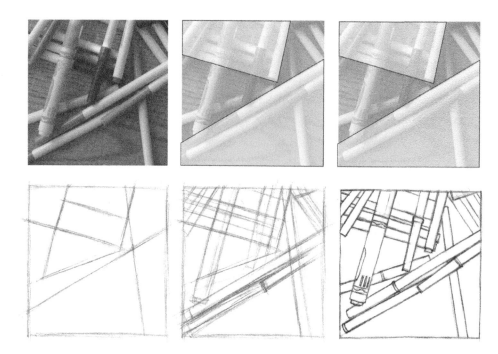

Traditionally, artists use negative space to align unrelated objects. Unfortunately, negative space is not an efficient or easy-to-use method for controlling overall structures. The black areas in Figure 6.2 show the negative space of the scene used in Figure 6.1. You can see that these black shapes are very irregularly structured and positioned. Even though the original pens have regular rectangular shapes, the space between them is fairly random. Furthermore, the negative space has lost the natural connection between the pens.

Figure 6.2

Negative space

For example, almost all pens in the scene have the same width, but the negative space does not reflect this fact. Drawing negative space directly is much harder and prone to problems. Using negative space for local adjustments is addressed later in this section.

Figure 6.3 is another example of grouped GSs found in a scene with many small objects. In the figure, different grouped GSs are identified and displayed. These dynamic shapes completely rely on the viewing position. Because of the many potential combinations, you may even find some very nicely grouped GSs in a busy scene. The right image of Figure 6.3 shows a fairly regularly shaped quadrilateral.

Technically, the more grouped GSs you identify, the more assistance you can get when you arrange objects on paper.

However, a rule of thumb is to create a big grouped GS and ignore the smaller ones. If you have too many groups, your task will become too complicated. This works against our initial purpose and will reduce the efficiency of your work. Another suggestion is to find grouped GSs that have special shapes, such as rectangles, right triangles, or equilaterals. These well-formed shapes can help you more than an average polygon does.

Figure 6.3

Three examples of grouping GSs in the same scene

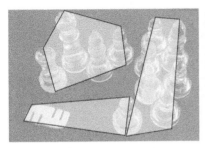 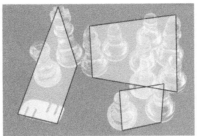 

Merging Objects with Overlapping Shapes

As you saw in the previous example, an object can be a part of different grouped GSs. This fact leads us to another interesting technique to lock the spatial relationship among multiple objects: overlapping shapes. An *overlapping shape* is created when two or more grouped GSs intersect, creating a new, interesting shape; that is, the overlapped area can be determined by two or more large shapes.

You may wonder why we need to do such extra work. In the previous chapters, we mainly used reference lines to lock key points and align structures. Reference lines are flexible and useful. But a line is not as visually noticeable as a polygon block. In other words, you can directly manipulate polygons to lock other shapes instead of using reference lines. Overlapping shapes is one of the techniques enabling you to quickly obtain a shape from other shapes. This trick is particularly useful for small but important graphical structures.

The left image of Figure 6.4 is a sample drawing of a human face. The image includes several small graphical features: eyes, nose, mouth, and so forth. If we don't use any knowledge of anatomy, these components can be considered different items. If we sketch these features independently, it will take a long time to adjust the position and size of each one in order to reach a correct overall configuration. To tie these features together, we can create two grouped GSs—one merges eyes and nose, and the other combines nose and mouth (see the center image of Figure 6.4). After we have these two big structures, the features are much easier for us to duplicate. Best of all, their intersection is the nose—that is, we lock the nose via these two shapes. Similarly, we can control the right eye with two other large polygons, as illustrated in the right image of Figure 6.4.

Figure 6.4

A face (left), and overlapping shapes to lock the nose (center) and control the right eye (right)

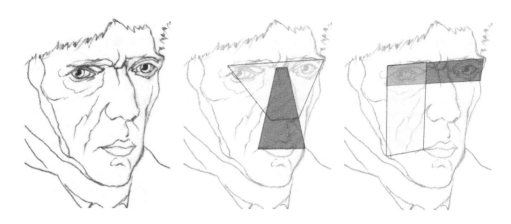

Figure 6.4

A face (left), and overlapping shapes to lock the nose (center) and control the right eye (right)

You may find many constructions of overlapping on your own. The overlap can be considered a bridge between the target shape and its neighboring shapes. Theoretically, using overlaps turns a small shape-controlling problem into a large shape-controlling problem. Another benefit is that we can control an irregularly shaped structure with two or more well-formed polygons. In this way, it is more intuitive to draw and control the target shape via regular ones.

Figure 6.5 illustrates one such scenario. The area between the mouth and nose in the figure can be approximated by an average quadrilateral, but that is prone to error. To control this complex polygon, we can find three better polygons containing the targeted area (see the three shaded areas in Figure 6.5). All three pieces are easy to duplicate, and their intersection is what we want to find.

Figure 6.5

Controlling an irregular shape via overlapping of regular shapes

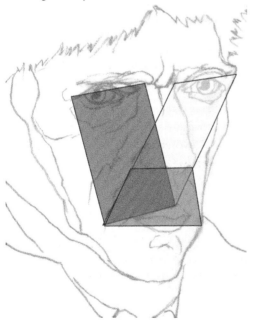

It should be pointed out that when we manipulate polygonal shapes directly, we depend on the technique of using reference lines. A polygonal shape is actually a collection of several key points and reference lines. Using polygons vs. reference lines and key points is pretty much like using multiplication vs. addition. Therefore, creating large polygons allows us to arrange graphical structures more efficiently. It can be considered an advanced level of using lines and points as previously described.

Using Virtual Skeletons for Fast Layout

Even if you have never taken a human anatomy class, you will still agree that the human skeleton truly governs a figure's form. For a complicated system such as the human body, the skeleton provides a simple but efficient tool for drawing a figure.

In a general scene that consists of random objects, there is no such natural skeleton. When we are partitioning the scene with a triangle mesh as in the ABC method, the edges of the mesh connect different items so that any detailed structure can be located by using these edges. In terms of functionality, a triangulation acts as a bone structure to host various objects.

If you look at a triangulation from a previous example, you may notice that most of the key points that were selected are on the boundaries of objects in order to control their sizes effectively. A real bone in anatomy, however, is always *inside* a muscle group—never on the boundary. This simple fact indicates that we can select internal key points of objects to set up a virtual skeleton system quickly—for example, a collection of reference lines that look like and act like a skeleton.

Here is how it is done: for every object in the scene, find its visual "center" point and then connect these center points with lines. These lines will act like the major bones in the scene. Additionally, use a line segment to replace a thin structure. These lines will control the sizes of individual objects.

The left image of Figure 6.6 illustrates one such example. In this scene, a few food cans have been placed on a table without any prearranged patterns. The hollow circles denote the center points of individual objects. The thick lines connecting the center points of these objects clearly look like a skeleton that controls the scene. Meanwhile, the thin lines in the image are more like bones inside the individual items. Put them together, and they represent a good virtual skeleton for the scene.

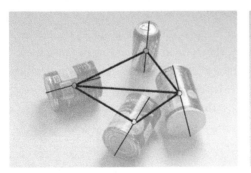 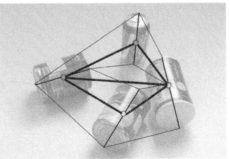

Figure 6.6

A scene with a virtual skeleton (left) and virtual skeleton assisted by triangulation (right)

You may find that using center points is an intuitive way to allocate positions of objects quickly. However, it is also hard to identify and visually trace them, because there are usually no visual markers for the center points. With these pros and cons in mind, you may use the virtual skeleton to help you find the triangulation; that is, you can use the end points and center points of the skeletal system as key points to create a polygonal partition over the scene. The right image of Figure 6.6 demonstrates a very low-resolution triangulation based on the virtual skeleton created in the left image. Although we have not used many key points (only three points per item to be exact), the mesh does a very good job in determining both the position and orientation of each item.

Using Negative Space to Adjust Small Structures

You've already learned that negative space is basically the blank area in a scene. Generally, the negative space contains many jagged shapes. Because the objects in a scene and the negative space between them are complementary, they fit each other perfectly, just like a jigsaw puzzle. Artists have used negative space for a long time for adjusting the positions between objects. Some book authors even suggest drawing negative space directly as an alternative way to drawing objects. The reality is that the irregularly shaped pieces in the negative space do not give us any obvious advantage in managing the overall scene. Therefore, in this book it is *not* recommended to draw objects by using negative space.

In the ABC method, a triangulation is mainly used to control various structures before adding detail. When we finalize a piece of artwork by drawing all the detailed features, you may still need some help in aligning small structures with the correct spatial relationships between them. You can always insert more key points if necessary, but an alternative way is to take advantage of the irregularity of negative space, because the negative space represents the association between two objects. Furthermore, the irregular shapes in the scene and on paper can be easily compared with each other.

Figure 6.7 shows a close-up of an area of a drawing in which the final detailed lines need to be finished. The left image shows the small features that need to be duplicated. The left-center image shows the final polygonal partitioning duplicated on paper. When you add detailed features, most of the time you replace polygonal edges with curves to depict small graphical features. The right-center image is such an attempt. In the top area of the image, curves are drawn. The right image shows the corresponding negative space in that region. It is immediately apparent from the negative-space image that the detailed features are not quite right, because the negative space doesn't appear to be very close to the original. This suggests that you need to adjust the curves at that location.

Figure 6.7

A zoomed-in area (left), duplicate of polygonal partitioning (left center), added detail in the top area (right center), and negative space in the top area (right)

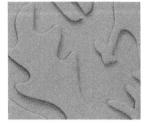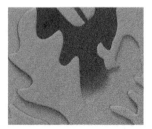

You may ask, "Why don't we use negative space in the earlier stages instead of in the last step?" Before the detail is drawn, all you have on paper are polygonal shapes with straight boundaries. These shapes can hardly be compared with negative space that has all kinds of smaller features. That is why we use the negative space only at the end. Honestly speaking, once you have a good triangulation on paper, all the graphical structures don't have a lot of space in which to move around. With the restriction of the triangulation, the detail you add can't be off too much. That's why negative space is used infrequently in the ABC method.

With the new techniques covered in this section, you should have more strategies for extracting and managing graphical structures. In the next section, you will see various demonstrations using all of the techniques that you have learned so far.

Demonstrations

In this section, you will draw various scenes by using the techniques you have learned so far. Because the drawing scenes are much more complicated than those used previously, you may find yourself frustrated in dealing with such a large amount of graphical information. Before starting a drawing, you always need to take a moment to look at the scene and identify the most significant structures. Ignore the detailed features at the beginning, and focus only on the major visual patterns. When you select techniques to apply to the scene, ask yourself the following questions: "How can I efficiently arrange these graphics on paper?" and "Which points are the most important in determining the overall structure?" Although you may make different decisions to process a still life, landscape, architecture, and 2D picture, the principle of the ABC method remains unchanged in the way that you draw them. You always follow these guidelines:

1. You always start with the big structures and then go down to smaller ones gradually.

2. You always use basic shapes to represent objects before adding detail.

3. You always search for any structural patterns in the scene that may help you to arrange the objects on paper.

4. You always use reference lines, angles, and triangulation to manage spatial information.

5. You always draw constructively. Everything you put on paper should have a clear purpose. Absolutely no aimless doodling is allowed.

In the previous chapters, all of the demonstrations were accompanied with partitioning illustrations. The images were shown with triangulation information so that you could learn how to use the ABC method. In reality, you cannot draw reference lines on a 3D scene. Even if you duplicate a 2D picture, it is strongly suggested that you not put any mark in the picture.

In the following demonstrations, basic triangulation is no longer displayed in the original scenes, unless it is needed to illustrate a new concept. You can still see how triangulation is used in actual drawing steps, however.

Fruit

In this setting, several pieces of fruit are placed in random order (see the left image of Figure 6.8). Each piece of fruit has a simple, rounded shape with smaller structures on

Figure 6.8

A scene composed
of fruit (left), its
virtual skeleton (left
center), small struc-
tures added (right
center), and the final
drawing (right)

top, so it is not hard to represent these pieces of fruit individually as circles. The hard part is to duplicate the overall configuration—that is, the position of each item in relation to the other items. If you start to select key points from the boundary as usual, you may find that most of the boundary curves are too smooth to track, which is true in this case. In contrast, the circular shapes of these pieces of fruit make their center points easy to iden-tify and the best tools for allocating position.

That being said, a virtual skeleton is sketched by using the center points, as shown in the left-center image of Figure 6.8. Because each of these circles (except the bottom-right one) basically touches its neighbor, the relative sizes of these circles are easy to determine. Therefore, circles can quickly be added to approximate each item. After this step, small structures are added to the tops of these circles, as illustrated in the right-center image of Figure 6.8. Because these detailed structures are pretty simple, creating any further trian-gulation to lock these shapes is optional. That is why you see that small circles and ovals are placed with little triangulation help. The last step is simply to confirm the structures of all items and finalize drawing lines.

Dumbbells

In this demonstration, you will draw two dumbbells, with one crossing over the other (see the left image of Figure 6.9). Technically, a dumbbell consists of three cylinders: a long handle and two short, heavy heads. To align these components efficiently, we can use the grouped graphical structure technique to merge all three cylinders into one big cylin-der. Therefore, to begin with, we just need to sketch two cylinders. The left-center image is the layout of these two simple cylinders on paper. Two rectangles are used to approximate them at this stage. Therefore, only a small number of lines are needed to determine the big picture of the scene. To confirm the relationship between these two cylinders, some reference lines are recommended. Because of the foreshortening of the top dumbbell, make sure the rectangle is tapered at one side.

Figure 6.9

A pair of dumbbells (left), sketch of two large cylinder structures (left center), detail structures added (right center), and the final drawing (right)

The next step is to divide each rectangle into several zones so that the three components can be placed. You may need to add some key points to control each component further. But grouping different components is more efficient. In the right-center image of the figure, you can see that the left head of the top dumbbell is merged with the two heads of the bottom dumbbell. The resulting simple shapes can greatly help us sketch all the ovals in the scene. The handles should be easy to draw. Negative space can also be used to ensure the correct sizes of the handles.

Leaves

In this demonstration, there are four leaves on vines climbing over an old tree (see the left image of Figure 6.10). Because of the nature of the subject, we don't have to spend a lot of time achieving a high degree of accuracy for these leaves. However, you may still want to achieve some accuracy in a short period of time. To do that, a simple and efficient way is to group the leaves in order to divide the paper into a few simple zones, as shown in the left-center image. The grouped graphical structures are approximated by simple polygons. Although not perfect, it is still a good way to control the accuracy of the overall construction of the scene.

After we have the big picture of the scene, it is pretty easy to add detailed curves for each leaf. An arc on top and a triangle shape on the bottom can be used to approximate each leaf. You don't have to use additional partitioning to determine these arcs and triangles, because each leaf is pretty much locked by the simple polygons on the paper. The right-center image is the scene sketched quickly.

Figure 6.10

Some leaves (left), some grouped graphical structures (left center), detail structures added (right center), and the final drawing (right)

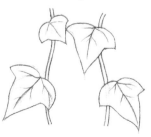

The whole scene contains much more detail than just the leaves. It is up to the artist to decide what to draw and what to ignore. When you look at a complicated scene like this, you should always decide first what you want to draw—that is, on what you want to focus. Otherwise, you may feel frustrated by the massive graphical patterns in front of you. Beginners must remember that you don't have to draw all the detailed texture in an observational drawing. Instead, ignoring the less important information will make the focused objects stand out more. The right image shows what I decided to focus on. Your decisions may be different, which is perfectly fine.

This demonstration shows you that the amount of effort you want to spend on triangulation depends on how much accuracy you want to achieve in your final drawing. In an outdoor drawing of landscapes, you should use a simple method to create an overall structure quickly on paper. However, if you want to duplicate a landscape masterpiece accurately, that is a different story altogether. Then you probably need to treat a tree leaf as seriously as a human face.

Chinese Landscape

Landscapes are popular subjects for observational drawing. When you take a vacation or visit any interesting spot, you can always take out your sketchbook and draw beautiful scenes quickly in addition to taking photos.

The left image of Figure 6.11 is a landscape that consists of a few trees, an old-fashioned Chinese bridge, and some distant hills. When you draw a landscape like this, the key is to arrange all of the objects on paper. The rest of the drawing (all the objects in detail) is pretty straightforward. You should not spend too much energy locking down smaller structures, because most natural objects such as bushes, trees, clouds, and mountains are randomly arranged.

The left-center image is the sketch of the overall structure. Only a few lines and shapes are needed to divide the paper into big zones. A complicated tree can be simply represented by a triangle—and the same goes for the bridge. After you confirm that the big picture looks okay, you can then add some additional shapes that represent each individual structure. Ovals are good for locking the sizes and locations of items you want to draw. The right-center image is the loose sketch at this step.

When you finalize every object, keep in mind that you don't have to draw every bit of detail you observe, especially for trees. The right image of Figure 6.11 is the final result of my drawing.

Because there are so many varieties of trees, drawing them is an interesting subject in fine art, and you can find many books on this topic. Please be aware that I consider myself an artist who draws trees poorly. This demonstration is not about teaching you how to draw trees but how to put various landscape objects on paper correctly and efficiently.

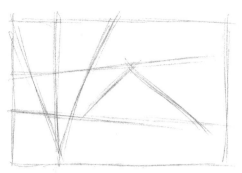

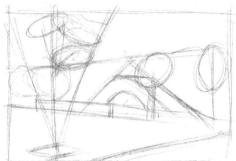

Figure 6.11

A landscape (top left), overall planning (top right), adding simple shapes for small structures (bottom left), and the final drawing (bottom right)

Stovetop

This example shows you how to draw a stovetop scene—a pressure cooker, several burners, and knobs (see the top left image of Figure 6.12). If you take a moment to look at this scene closely, you will find many oval structures. In addition, all the burners and knobs are arranged in a grid-like arrangement on a rectangular stovetop.

Figure 6.12

A stovetop setting (top left), overall planning (top right), adding structures (bottom left), and the final drawing (bottom right)

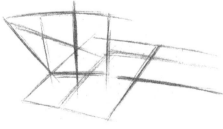

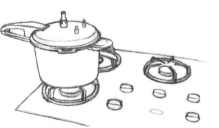

With this observation in mind, you need to arrange the pan and the stovetop first. Sketching the stovetop is pretty simple because it is already a rectangular shape. The pressure cooker is a union of a big cylinder and a triangular-shaped handle. The top right image of Figure 6.12 shows the sketch. Obviously, you can merge the handle, the lid, and the pressure cooker to create a grouped GS. Merging items together is an efficient way to control proportions and locations of these items corresponding to each other. Typically, you can obtain useful GSs by merging neighboring structures. When you draw a complicated scene, this should be your must-use strategy.

Next we need to add some big structures—in this case, various ovals. Because the paper is already divided into small pieces by polygons in the previous step, it is not necessary to divide these polygons further. Structures can be added directly. The bottom left image of Figure 6.12 shows the result of this step. After that, it is just a matter of time to draw all the detailed features of the scene. The bottom right image of Figure 6.12 represents the final piece of work.

You may notice that the ovals of the front and right burners look odd. Because of the close proximity of the camera to the subject, these two burners are distorted. If you draw the real 3D scene, the long axes of these ovals should be more parallel than they appear in this image.

Fruit and Container

Fruit is one of the most popular still-life subjects for artists to practice drawing. In this demonstration, there are several individual and grouped items: bananas and apples in a flat bowl, a red apple standing alone, and a big blender container (see the top left image of Figure 6.13).

First, let's sketch this scene with a few simple polygons. When you have multiple small items, such as apples, it is always a good idea to consider them as one big individual item. With this strategy, all the bananas are also viewed as a single item. Therefore, we can use simple polygons to approximate these grouped GSs. To ensure correct proportional relationships among these polygons, reference lines are used, as indicated in the top right image of Figure 6.13.

Next, it is pretty straightforward to add bananas in the triangle area at the right, apples and the bowl in the triangle at the bottom, the red apple on the left side, and the container in the polygon at the top. When you sketch apples in the bowl, just make sure that their sizes are relatively similar. You don't have to use any key points to lock their positions, because they are already restricted within a very small triangle. The bottom left image of Figure 6.13 is the output of this process. The bottom right image of Figure 6.13 is the completed drawing.

Figure 6.13

Fruit and container (top left), partition for groups (top right), adding structures (bottom left), and the final drawing (bottom right)

Messy Boats

Sometimes a scene can be very messy: different-sized objects randomly mixed with various small items. The top left image of Figure 6.14 is one such example. In this case, several Asian fishing boats are packed together with many smaller items. In real life, it is probably not necessary to arrange and draw such a messy scene as accurately as observed in life. But for the sake of this exercise, you will learn how to manage such a chaotic scene on paper efficiently.

The major objects in this scene are boats. But they are obviously positioned at random. To capture this configuration, a few lines are used to divide the scene into several large zones (see the top right image of Figure 6.14). When a scene has many graphical elements, make sure you pick the most important ones and focus on them. The rest can be drawn loosely or even ignored. In this example, the front boat and the two boats at the right side are the ones to focus on.

Next, more lines are added to further the existing polygons' partition. Because there are so many possible ways to create reference lines here, you usually insert lines at the focused areas in order to be able to draw structures in these regions. The bottom left image displays one such step. Most of the reference lines added here are directly selected from the real objects. At this point, all the major boats are locked so that the detailed structures can be drawn straightaway. If you feel it is still too early to draw small items, you may add one more round of reference lines. There is no restriction on the number of steps in the ABC method. It's simply based on your needs.

Figure 6.14

Messy boats (top left), a quick partition (top right), further partition (bottom left), and the final drawing (bottom right)

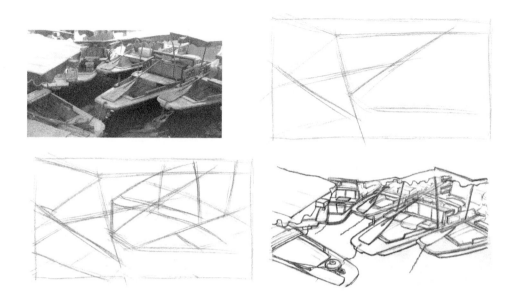

The bottom right image shows the final result. Some unimportant details are ignored for obvious reasons. It is always a good idea not to fill a paper completely when you draw a very busy scene.

Women's Shoes

This is a complicated example, although it seems rather easy. The top left image of Figure 6.15 shows a pair of women's shoes. Each shoe contains many structures that are prone to drawing errors. Curves in each component are so dramatic that you have to draw them pretty accurately for them to look good. In the previous chapter, you already learned how to use key points to lock each landmark on a single shoe. In this demonstration, you will learn how to draw similar objects more efficiently.

Because there are so many small but important structures in the shoes, it is a good idea to group them and use big polygons to establish an overall plan. The top right image of Figure 6.15 shows a sketch of a few such grouped GSs. You may find that some GSs have very nice parallel edges. When you identify and group structures, you need to pick those with special patterns first, because they are the easiest to duplicate.

After we partition the scene with these polygonal shapes on paper, we can immediately add more grouped GSs and reference lines to further divide the whole scene into smaller pieces (see the bottom left image of Figure 6.15). At this point, you probably see a pair of shoes in a collection of straight lines. If you compare the single-shoe drawing demonstration in Chapter 5 (see Figure 5.15) with this example, you will find that using grouped GSs or polygons is much more efficient than adding individual key points. That makes perfect sense, because each polygon you draw carries with it multiple key points and reference lines. Putting one polygon down on paper is equivalent to allocating several key points and reference lines. Of course, this strategy should be used only after you master the basic skills of creating individual key points and reference lines. Otherwise, you might find it difficult to create the polygons correctly.

The bottom right image of Figure 6.15 is the final drawing after all curves are drawn on the top of the polygons.

Figure 6.15

Figure 6.15

A pair of women's shoes (top left), some grouped graphical structures (top right center), detail structures added (bottom left), and the final drawing (bottom right)

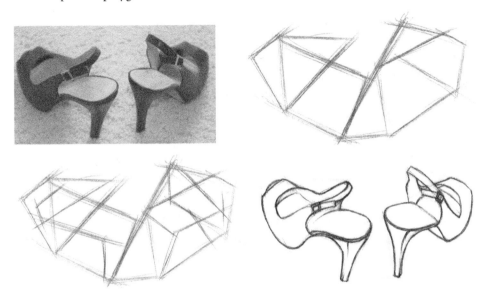

Group of Dancers

You will learn how to draw human figures by using both anatomy knowledge and dynamic graphical structures in Chapter 8, "Special Techniques for Drawing Human Bodies." But in this demonstration, you will see how the ABC method helps you draw dynamic figures *without* using anatomy. This is a perfect method for those who have not yet studied anatomy.

The top left image of Figure 6.16 is a photo of dancers on stage. Each one has a dynamic pose, and the costumes have rich colors and detail. The whole scene is very busy, and it looks as messy as the boat example we drew earlier. But unlike boats, humans have special structures that we must draw accurately.

To start planning this scene, four big virtual bones are used to represent the four figures in the center of the image. The top right image of Figure 6.16 is the simple virtual skeleton employed. Even if you don't have any knowledge of anatomy, you should be able to see such a single-line "skeleton." Reference lines are also used here to secure the proportions between the virtual skeletons.

Figure 6.16

Group of dancers (top left), partition with virtual skeletons (top right), adding large structures (bottom left), and the final drawing (bottom right)

The next step is to arrange structures for each figure. Because no anatomy knowledge is assumed, we cannot use any assistance such as rib cages or sticklike structures that are traditionally used by artists. Instead, we must find dynamic patterns from the scene.

Actually, finding these patterns is quite easy if you look at each body component of a dancer. For example, the leftmost dancer has two hands in the air, and her skirt is swirling in the middle. Each hand and arm can be merged with the skirt to form a large triangle. Similarly, we can find a triangle that combines her leg and foot and skirt. The bottom left image of Figure 6.16 is the sketch of the grouped GS. Obviously, the same treatment is applied to all of the other dancers.

The polygons obtained so far are good enough for us to add all kinds of detail. Drawing elements of the human body such as arms, hands, and feet might be challenging if you have never drawn them before. Just treat them as regular objects, and approach them as we have in the previous cases. The only difference is that you might need to do so slowly to achieve accuracy. You can use more reference lines if you are having difficulty. The polygons created so far control the major structures of the dancers and their poses. Before adding details, you need to double-check their accuracy. Once you start to add details, it is very difficult to change the major structures already created.

Adding detail based on established structures usually doesn't involve arrangement for large structure. It is a task of drawing small individual items. You may adjust or modify them fairly easily without affecting the major structures on the paper. The bottom right image is my result for the final drawing.

You have seen demonstrations on various complicated scenes in this section. When you are drawing multiple objects, quickly connecting them with references and/or polygons is an effective way to tie them together in order to control their spatial relationships. After you have created a good partitioning on paper, drawing is simplified by handling individual objects.

Exercises

GROUPED GSs

1. Find five photos or real scenes that contain many structures. For each object in a scene, identify at least two grouped GSs that contain the object. Draw all these grouped GSs only.

2. Place many small objects, such as clips or pens, randomly on a table. Find the grouped GSs and sketch them. Rearrange the objects and do it again. Repeat this exercise five times.

SHAPE OVERLAPPING

3. Set up a scene with at least five items. For each item, create some grouped GSs so that their overlap is (roughly) the targeted item.

VIRTUAL SKELETONS

4. Find a few random objects and put them together without any pattern. Sketch the virtual skeleton in the scene.

NEGATIVE SPACE

5. Set up a messy scene that contains some fabrics. After sketching polygons for their main structures, draw the detailed features by using the negative space method for confirmation and adjustment of the small features. Reset the scene and do it again. Repeat this exercise five times.

CHAPTER 7

Using Advanced Techniques

Fine art is knowledge made visible.

—GUSTAVE COURBET (1819-1877), FRENCH REALIST PAINTER

With the advancement of your drawing skill, you now need to move up to the next level of processing spatial information and controlling shapes. Although the ABC method is founded on a basic knowledge of geometry and computer graphics principles, the simple concepts employed in the method do not prevent development of advanced techniques for managing graphical structures.

In the preceding chapter, we started to manipulate shapes directly rather than relying on key points and reference lines. Although key points and reference lines are fundamental for determining shapes, directly processing shapes can be done much faster and more efficiently—if we do it accurately.

In this chapter, you will learn some of the more advanced techniques for handling shapes for improved drawing. You will also work through demonstrations of drawing various objects by using the new techniques. In particular, the following topics are addressed:

- Working with curved triangles and polygons

- Drawing a group of ovals

- Using shadows and shadow maps

- Using rhythms for fast partitioning

- Trading off between accuracy and speed

Working with Curved Triangles and Polygons

A triangle or polygon has several edges, and each edge is a straight-line segment. As a method for connecting two points, a straight line is simple to understand and easy to use without ambiguity. However, from the demonstrations and exercises in the previous chapters, you probably already noticed that a straight line is not very efficient when drawing structures that involve curves. Often we have to employ multiple lines to approximate a piece of a curve in order to get an accurate drawing. This issue can be explained and improved based on the mathematical properties of lines.

In mathematics, a straight line is a *linear polynomial*, and it has very limited use when dealing with nonlinear curves. A better way for fast approximation would be to use non-linear curves such as quadratic or *cubic polynomials*.

LINEAR AND NONLINEAR POLYNOMIALS

A linear polynomial is expressed as $y = ax + b$, and its graphical shape is a straight line. The simplest nonlinear polynomial is a *quadratic polynomial*, or $y = ax^2 + bx + c$. Its shape is a *parabola*. The maximum power, or exponent, in a polynomial is called the *degree of the polynomial*. The degree of a linear polynomial is one (1). The degree of a parabola is two (2), and the degree of a cubic polynomial is three (3).

In terms of appearance, the degree of a polynomial reflects the softness of the corresponding curve. A straight line (linear polynomial) is unbendable. A parabola can bend only once. A cubic polynomial can bend twice, and so on (see Figure 7.1).

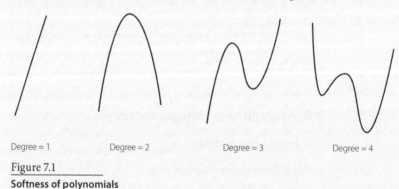

Degree = 1   Degree = 2   Degree = 3   Degree = 4

Figure 7.1
Softness of polynomials

Curved Triangles, Polygons, and Triangulation

Nonlinear approximation has been widely used in many graphic software programs as a basic method for creating curves. For example, Adobe's Creative Suite (CS) products use cubic Bézier, a specially formatted polynomial, to generate complicated shapes. Besides the high level of efficiency, nonlinear polynomials also allow us to use smooth curves and thus avoid the sharp corners that exist in polygons.

Obviously, using nonlinear polynomials is an easy task for computers but a hard job for artists. We should never expect an artist to perform complicated polynomial calculations in order to create a curve. To make a nonlinear mechanism work for drawing purposes, some modifications and restrictions are necessary.

First, we will use only the simplest nonlinear curves: quadratic polynomials or parabolas. For easy control, we don't want a curve that can be bent several times. Compared with higher-degree polynomials, a parabola is not powerful or soft enough to approximate a wavelike shape. But using multiple pieces of parabola segments together, or piecewise polynomials, will solve this problem. A *piecewise polynomial* is a natural extension of a polygon, which concatenates polynomial segments piece by piece. In CG, piecewise (low-degree) curves are widely used to create long and complicated curves. The left image of Figure 7.2 shows how a piecewise parabola is able to approach a wavelike pattern marked by hollow circles. In the image, solid circles represent the joints between two adjacent parabolas.

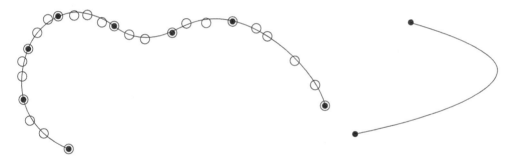

Figure 7.2

Approximating a large number of points with a piecewise parabola (left) and avoiding a sharp-turned curve (right)

Because of the use of multiple pieces, there is a second restriction. We don't use a single, sharply bent curve (see the right image of Figure 7.2). It is much harder for a person to duplicate such curves as compared to flat ones. So, we use a piecewise approach—using multiple flat curve segments—instead.

In Chapter 3, "Drawing with the ABC Method," you saw a simple example of using curved triangulation/polygons. You will be introduced to a nonlinear treatment for faster processing of structures. A *curved triangle* is a triangle that is allowed to have curves for its three sides. Similarly, by using curves instead of lines, we get the concept of curved polygons and *curved triangulation*. Figure 7.3 shows some simple examples of these new models.

We use this nonlinear treatment solely for the speed and convenience of handling complicated shapes. Unlike a line, a single curve can approximate more than two key points pretty well. Therefore, this technique is very powerful in the initial stage, when you sketch the big structures of a scene. However, some approximation errors are inevitable because not all key points will align perfectly on a curve. You will need to make some corrections in a later stage.

Figure 7.3

A curved triangle
(left) and a curved
polygon (right)

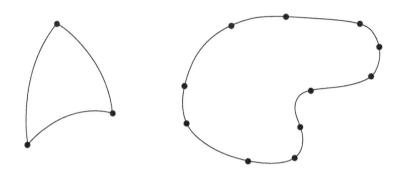

The first two images of Figure 7.4 show two steps of a curved triangulation on a photo presented earlier, in Chapter 5, "Drawing Complicated Objects." We want to supplement this simple scene with key points. In the left image, a large curved triangle is used to approximate the area of interest. The large, black circles are the key points in this step. The center image represents further subdivision as we add two more key points (marked by small, black circles). Two thin curves are also added. With these few points, all major structures are identified and ready to be extracted for drawing. For comparison, the right image of Figure 7.4 shows the key points and corresponding linear triangulation used earlier in Chapter 5. You can see that curved triangles are more efficient for representing structures than traditional triangles.

Figure 7.4

Initial step of a
curved triangulation
(left), refinement of
the triangulation
(center), and the
traditional triangu-
lation (right)

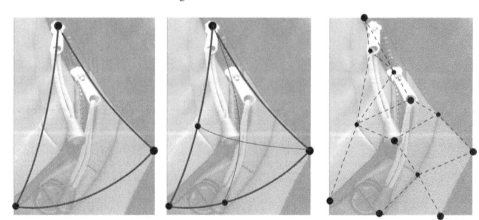

Quadratic Bézier Curves

Surely a parabola is more flexible than a straight line. But it is also ambiguous. Given a pair of end points, you can create an infinite number of parabolas passing between these two points. So, how do we determine and control the curve? Bézier schemes in modern CG provide a good solution by letting users easily manipulate the curve. In Chapter 1, "Understanding the Relationship between Math and Art," you were shown the construction of a cubic Bézier curve. The idea works exactly the same way for the quadratic Bézier, which is basically a parabola.

Here is how a quadratic Bézier is determined. Let's look at the line segments AB and BC in the left image of Figure 7.5. Segments AB and BC together are called the *control polygon* of the curve we want to create. We want to form a nice curve starting at A, ending at C, and tangent to the lines AB and BC at the end points. To do that, we use a midpoint subdivision process: we determine the midpoint D of AB, and the midpoint E of line BC, and then find the midpoint F of DE. Now we have a point F and two smaller-sized control polygons ADF and FEC. Point F, which is the point on the curve we want, is considered the midpoint of the curve. We then replace the original control polygon ABC by two sub-control polygons: ADF and FEC. We can apply this process on these smaller control polygons to obtain more points on the curve as well as refine them. If we repeat this process a few more times, the subcontrol polygons generated will quickly approach the Bézier curve, which is displayed by the dashed curve.

POLYGON VS CONTROL POLYGON

The geometry term "polygon" used in this book represents a *closed* 2D shape that bounded by line segments. However, the "control polygon" used by Bézier curves is not necessary closed in general. We cannot change the name of this widely used computer graphics term, although it may cause some confusion for you. Please remember that "control polygon" is used only for constructing Bézier curves, while a "polygon" is used to represent and control general graphical structures in this book.

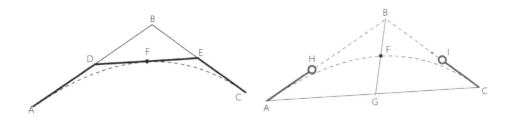

Figure 7.5

A subdivision process of a quadratic Bézier curve (left), and controlling the curve with end points and tangent lines (right)

This so-called subdivision construction process is how a Bézier curve is rendered with today's CG software. It also provides an easy way to control the shape of the curve via a simple control polygon. An alternative way to use a control polygon is with two end points and two tangent lines (see the right image of Figure 7.5). A *tangent* or tangent line of a curve at a particular point is a line that just touches the curve at that point. The circles in the image represent the handles of tangent lines at the end points. Most graphic software programs provide this method for users to create and edit curves.

The right image of Figure 7.5 provides a guide on how "fat" a Bézier should be drawn on paper if we are given two tangent lines and positions. In the image, B is the intersecting point of the two tangents. Point F on the curve is the midpoint of line BG, where G is the midpoint of AC.

Drawing a Group of Ovals

An *oval* is one of the two basic shapes we need to conquer. In many cases, you will draw various ovals in the same scene. As we discussed earlier, drawing an oval is difficult, and putting a group of ovals together is definitely much more challenging because of the spatial relationship between ovals that also needs to be addressed. This section presents two techniques for handling multiple ovals.

Determining the Axes of an Oval

In Chapter 4, "Drawing Simple Objects," you learned how to acquire the proportion of an oval by using midpoints of the oval. The four midpoints are able to determine the proportion as well as the orientations of both axes of the oval. But this method depends on how accurate you can eyeball the midpoints on the oval. Allocating midpoints can be tricky if there is no obvious marker or visual reference on the oval. In this section, you will learn an alternative method for obtaining the axes of an oval.

Acquiring both axes of an oval from a scene is the hard part for many people. Figure 7.6 shows a common problem that a beginner may encounter in constructing ovals. The left image is a rough sketch of a small digital camera with its lens retracted. The oval represents the location and size of the lens. Many people believe that the major axis is oriented in a vertical direction, as displayed in the left image. The result seems okay, or at least not too bad. But in the right image, the extended lens forms a cylinder. Now you probably see that the cylinder lens is not quite right. What went wrong?

Figure 7.6

An incorrect sketch of a small digital camera with lens retracted (left) and lens extended (right)

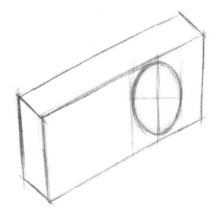
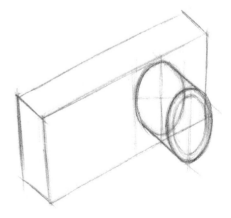

In mathematics, an oval can be viewed as an intersection of a plane and a sphere, a cylinder, or a cone. The short axis of an oval is *always* parallel to the direction (or normal vector) that the cutting plane faces (see Figure 7.7). In the image, the white vertical rectangle represents a cylinder. The gray deformed rectangle is a cutting plane that intersects the cylinder and creates a (dark shaded) oval. The direction of the cutting plane is represented by an arrow that is attached to the plane. Understanding this geometric principle will allow you to draw ovals easily and correctly.

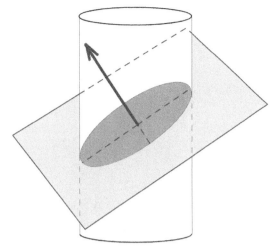

Figure 7.7

The short axis is always parallel to the direction that the cutting plane faces

NORMAL VECTOR OF A 3D PLANE

In 3D space, you can position a plane or a piece of paper to face a given direction. This direction is always perpendicular to the plane, and it is called the *normal vector* of the plane in geometry.

Some art books teach readers to identify the short axis via the axis of a cylinder. But this is true only if the cutting plane is perpendicular to the cylinder—and that is not always the case. Figure 7.7 already showed you those situations where the cutting planes are not perpendicular to the axis of the cylinder. In this case, you must use the normal vector of the cutting plane as the short axis of the resulting oval.

Drawing Cross Sections

The left image of Figure 7.8 is a drawing that you will find in many perspective drawing books. These ovals are cross sections of a cylinder. You can find such ovals in a transparent bottle of water. Unfortunately, determining proportions with the perspective theory is a tedious task. You have to set up vanishing points and then determine how a square is distorted in perspective before you can actually draw an oval, as illustrated by the left image of Figure 7.8.

Figure 7.8

Drawing cross
sections with the
perspective theory
(left) and a new way
developed from
geometry (right)

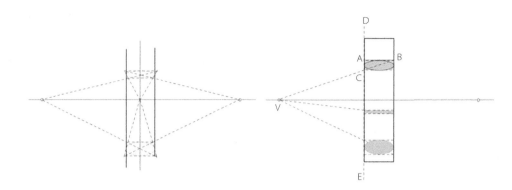

Actually, there is an easier way to complete this task—a more intuitive trick derived directly from geometry. The right image of Figure 7.8 shows a side view of the setting: a cylinder is in front of your eye. Assume that there is a cross section (circle) of the cylinder, and the line segment AB represents the circle in the side view. For convenience, we put the image plane directly at point A. The image place is placed vertically so you can only see it as a line in this side view. We represent it as line segment DE in the image. Now we can take a look at what happens when the cross section is projected onto the image plane. Obviously, point A is projected on itself because this point is already on the image plane. But point B is projected onto point C, the intersecting point of lines DE and VB. This fact simply tells us that AC is the thickness of the cross section AB on the image plane. This is an extremely important property of cross sections. It shows us that the image of a cross section—that is, an oval on the image plane—has a proportion ratio of AB/AC. In other words, points A, B, and C define the bounding box of the oval you see.

Now, imagine you rotate the whole scene 90 degrees around the axis of the cylinder and that you are in the position of point V. In other words, the side view becomes the front view. The cylinder remains the same shape under this rotation, and so does the ratio of AC/AB. This indicates that the oval defined by the side view is exactly what we see in the front view!

SOME LIMITATIONS ON THE VIEWING ANGLE

The method of drawing a cross section is derived based on the assumption that viewing rays can be cast out from the viewing point in any direction. In reality, human eyes cannot do that. You have a very limited range for seeing objects in front of your eyes without rolling your eyeballs or even turning your head. So, the technique works well within a small viewing range (about 30 degrees above and below the view level). If you want to draw a cross section high above your head, you have to turn your head up. In this case, the image plane has changed, because it is always aligned perfectly in front of your eyes. Therefore, this method no longer holds true. If you still use this method, the results may not look as realistic as you see.

With this fact in mind, we can easily draw any cross section without using traditional time-consuming processes shown in the left image of Figure 7.8. In the right image of Figure 7.8, two more cross sections are drawn by simply shooting lines from point V and obtaining the intersection points and bounding boxes, which allows you to draw ovals right away. It is that simple!

Using Shadow Maps

CG artists often use a tool called a *shadow map* to indicate shapes and locations of shadows prior to rendering. Figure 7.9 is an example of a shadow map indicating various lines on the face. The shadow map is typically used when an artist does not have enough time to render a quick pose, although the shadow map itself is also a beautiful drawing style.

Figure 7.9

Shadow map in a portrait drawing

When you have multiple objects positioned under a strong light source, you will see many randomly shaped shadows on the surface as well as on the nearby objects. These shadows immediately connect objects and thus provide us with a very good way to merge graphical structures. Figure 7.10 is an example of several pieces of fruit under direct sunlight. Obviously, the boundaries of the shadows are a good reference for us to allocate the position of individual items. If you want, you can even consider these shadows as virtual objects, just like negative space.

SHADOWS

Two major types of shadows are created by light: cast shadows and core shadows. A *cast shadow*, as its name indicates, is the shadow directly cast by an object from a strong light source. Usually, a cast shadow has very clear/hard boundary lines. A *core shadow*, also called a *terminator*, is the shadow that results from two light sources coming from opposite directions. In a typical scenario, a major light source lights an object. If the background is bright, the object will receive reflecting light from the direction opposite the major light source. A core shadow is the darkest part of an object, and its boundaries are soft and thick. In Figure 7.10, you can see the arc-shaped dark area on the honeydew melon. That is the core shadow. The pears and apples also have core shadows.

Figure 7.10

Fruit under direct sunlight

Besides helping us to link objects together, shadows are also a powerful way to represent objects realistically. If an object is drawn using only outlines without shadow, rendering, textures, or detail, it will look like a 2D cartoon drawing and not like a realistic rendering of a 3D object. Rendering is beyond the scope of this book, but you can still use some detailed shadows or textures to illustrate the 3D depth of an object.

Figure 7.11

Apple with reflected textures (left), initial structure on paper (center left), placing reflections (center right), and the final drawing (right)

The left image of Figure 7.11 is a close-up view of an apple displaying various reflections on its surface. These textures, treated as shadows or even regular structures, can be extracted and sketched on paper. The next three images of Figure 7.11 show the three major steps in drawing the apple and its reflection shadow map. We start with a simple circle for the body of the apple and a polygon for the bottom. We use a long curve to indicate the major shadow pattern in the center. Next, we construct a few small reflection spots by using polygons. The last step is to draw the final lines with smooth curves.

Shadows are free gifts from light sources. In studio drawing, you can always add some strong lights to a scene to take advantage of the benefits brought about by additional shadows. So, don't ignore them next time you draw.

Using Rhythms for Partitioning

Rhythm is a term used in music for the pattern of sound movement through time and space. The concept is also used in the visual arts to indicate patterns of repeated shapes. When you draw a large number of objects, it is always a good idea to find any explicit or hidden pattern among them that can help with shape management. You may find such patterns easily in man-made objects or designed arrangements such as computer keyboards, windows in a wall, and trees in a garden. However, this doesn't happen all the time because, in most scenes, objects appear randomly.

In the previous chapters, you learned several techniques for bringing random structures together. In this section, you will learn one more technique that you can put into your tool set. When a scene includes many objects, you almost always find many repeated visual patterns across the scene. For example, vertical lines will appear here and there, and so will horizontal lines. If objects are of similar types, you will see a common pattern. Even though these patterns are not perfectly aligned, they still give us additional help for handling spatial structures.

The left image of Figure 7.12 is a parking lot scene. Several tall palm trees are standing vertically in the foreground. Although they are not evenly spaced, these vertical lines will help you partition your drawing into several zones. You can also find long horizontal lines derived from the curbs, parked cars, and distant trees (see the center-left image of Figure 7.12). After you have these vertical and horizontal lines on paper, the drawing task is simplified into merely filling in detailed structures in each divided zone. You may notice that these lines actually serve as grids, just as in the grid method. The difference is that the lines created in the ABC method are dynamic and needs-based.

Besides the vertical and horizontal lines, you can clearly find other structures such as automobiles and trees in this landscape. Because of their relative sizes in the scene, you don't have to use polygons to approximate each one accurately. In the center-right image of Figure 7.12, circles/ovals are used to represent these smaller items. These repeated patterns or rhythms enable us to manage them easily on paper.

Adding the detail should be an easy job because each automobile is specifically located. Because there are many automobiles, you don't have to treat all of them equally. Instead, spend more time on the most important spots and concentrate on drawing them accurately. For the rest of the areas, you can draw them in roughly or even ignore them. The right image of Figure 7.12 is the result of such treatment.

Figure 7.12

A parking lot scene (top left), vertical and horizontal rhythms in the scene (top right), smaller items being placed (bottom left), and the actual drawing (bottom right)

Exploring Trade-Offs between Accuracy and Speed

So far, we haven't placed any time restrictions on your drawing. You have had as much as time you needed to finish your projects. However, you should know that speed is also a key factor in measuring your drawing skills, although accuracy is more important for observational drawing.

The ABC method teaches you how to achieve a high degree of accuracy with different techniques for structural extraction and manipulation. Every step takes time, and accuracy is generally proportional to the time you spend drawing. However, not all objects require the same level of accuracy. For example, when you draw a tree or mountain, you don't have to waste time on the accuracy of all the small details. Having a good sketch of major structures plus some faked detail will result in a decent drawing. The preceding parking lot drawing is a good example of this.

Keep in mind that drawing is something of an engineering problem. You need to manage how to achieve the maximum results within a limited amount of time. Therefore, you always spend most of your valuable time on the most important parts of the drawing, while sacrificing accuracy for less-important areas.

The five new techniques presented in this chapter are some of the advanced procedures that you can apply in the ABC method. They will help you to further improve your drawing efficiency and quality. Furthermore, they are more than just artistic theories. They are actual techniques that you can apply to all of your drawing in the future. That being said, get ready for drawing along with the demonstrations that follow.

Demonstrations

In the following demonstrations, the newly introduced techniques in this chapter are used first, even if some old techniques are also applicable. Various subjects are chosen in order to cover a wide range of topics.

Flowers

Organic objects such as flowers always contain many visual patterns with smooth curves. These objects form dynamic graphical structures that enable us to apply various techniques to arrange them intelligently. In this demonstration, the main techniques applied are the creation of curved triangles and polygons. Figure 7.13 is a garden flower that we will be drawing.

Figure 7.13
A garden flower

The flower in the picture has rich and beautiful structures. You can easily find various useful patterns here: repeated structures, oval shapes, triangle configurations, and so forth. The white petals that form a large curved triangle are the focus of this picture. The left image of Figure 7.14 shows the starting point of the drawing process. It contains primarily a curved triangle that locks the big shapes of the white petals. The two lines in the middle sketch the cone-shaped body.

The next step is to organize the smaller structures. In the body part, we can identify a few triangular grouped structures. They also form a rhythm to partition the body part, as shown in the center-left image of Figure 7.14.

Figure 7.14
Starting with a curved triangle (left), locking structures in the body (center left), placing all structures (center right), and the final drawing (right)

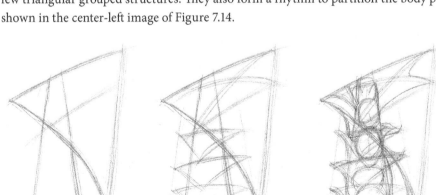

After we have constructed this layout for the major structures, it is time to sketch the detailed features. There are many textures on the petals, but you should ignore them at this time. Just use some simple shapes to represent each structure. Ovals and curved triangles are useful for this task. The center-right image of Figure 7.14 is the result of all of the structures outlined here.

After confirming the correctness of individual parts and their relationships, we finalize the shapes with smooth curves. Some textures are also added selectively to help define the flower. The right image of Figure 7.14 is the completed drawing for this demonstration.

Van Gogh's Face

You drew this face in a lesson at the very beginning of this book. Now you will use the new techniques you've learned to redraw the facial area. The top-left image of Figure 7.15 is our drawing target. In this demonstration, we are interested in only the face—the most difficult part of the portrait.

To start the process, a curved polygon is used to lock the overall shape. The curves are obtained by ignoring all the small, bumpy details. If you have difficulty seeing a curved polygon, ask yourself the following question: "If I am allowed to use only four or five simple curves to outline this face, what curves will they be?" You can use all kinds of reference lines and angles to ensure accuracy. The top-center image of Figure 7.15 shows the result of this step.

Figure 7.15

Van Gogh's face (top left), starting with a curved polygon (top center), partitioning with reference lines (top right), locking all major features (bottom left), sketching all features (bottom center), and the final drawing (bottom right)

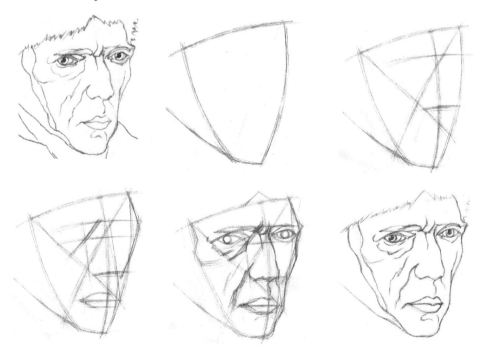

When you draw a face, you may notice that the eyes and eyebrows are symmetrical, even if you've never had an anatomy class. This fact allows us to place an eyebrow line or eye line quickly on the face. You may place a nose line to indicate the bottom location of the nose. These lines are important when drawing portraits. Besides, it is also helpful to find some dynamic references, such as the cross lines in the top-right image of Figure 7.15. These are obtained by shooting lines from the top-left and top-right corners to the left side of nose. The big wrinkle at the left side of the nose is the main reason for creating such reference lines. The centerline is also added here. Unless you draw a perfect front view of a face, a centerline is *always* curved as it is appears in the top-right image of Figure 7.15. One common mistake made by beginners is drawing a straight centerline for a nonfrontal view of a face. This will result in the misplacement of the mouth later.

The next step is to keep partitioning by adding more structural lines. We add the eye and mouth lines. When you are looking for the next structure to add to the drawing, always ask this question: "What is the most important feature that is not yet on paper?" If you are able to answer this question promptly, you will never stop moving your pencil on the paper. The bottom-left image of Figure 7.15 is another snapshot after this refinement.

Adding all detailed features is the next big step. Because you already subdivided the facial area into various zones, it is a fairly easy job to know the location of each facial feature. Drawing the eyes, nose, and mouth is a hard job because of the high degree of accuracy that is required. In Chapter 4, "Drawing Simple Objects," you learned how to draw them individually with polygons. You may use that technique now to draw all of them, or you can apply the new curved polygon technique to accomplish the same task. Spend more time on the eyes, because they are the most important feature of the face. The bottom-center image of Figure 7.15 is the sketch of all the features.

Finalizing all structural lines and fixing some minor mistakes are the tasks to accomplish in the last step. The right image of Figure 7.15 is the finished result.

Digital Camera

This demonstration is primarily designed to show you techniques for drawing ovals. The top-left image of Figure 7.16 is of a digital camera with an extended lens. The camera can be considered a cubic body with a few short cylinders. The overall structure is not complicated, but drawing the ovals is pretty tricky, as you saw earlier in this chapter. A quick analysis of the ovals is given in the top-center image of Figure 7.16. In this image, the oval axes are displayed as well as the direction of each face (marked by arrows).

To start the drawing, we sketch a polygon for the body of the camera and place a big oval for the base of the camera's lens (see the top-right image of Figure 7.16). Numerous reference lines are used to help establish the proportions of the body. For the base oval, its minor/short axis is parallel to the two edges of the top face of the body, as indicated by arrows in the top-center image of Figure 7.16. After the minor axis is determined, the major axis is simply the perpendicular direction of the minor axis. Make sure the axes look okay, because they are fundamental in determining how the other ovals for the lens are structured.

Figure 7.16

A digital camera (top left), a structural analysis (top center), starting with the body and base of the lens (top right), adding more oval structures (bottom left), sketching all of the features (bottom center), and the final drawing (bottom right)

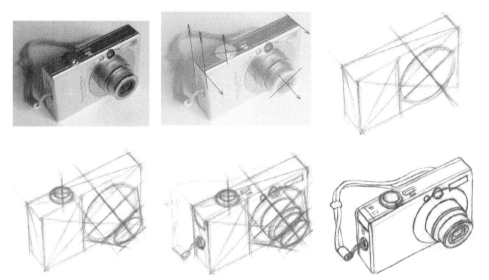

There are a couple of ovals in the lens part. All of them have the same axes directions and proportions because they are cross sections of a cone structure extending from the base oval. To lock the location of the oval at the tip of the lens, we construct a cone by drawing two side lines. Ovals are also created for the small shutter button on top of the rectangle of the camera body. The bottom-left image of Figure 7.16 shows the result of this step.

The remaining job is mainly sketching each oval in the lens. Because the top and bottom ovals are established, the ovals in between are not too hard to draw. All other miscellaneous parts are also added in this step. The bottom-center image of Figure 7.16 is the drawing that results at this point.

If everything is okay, the last step is to draw clean lines for all structures. The bottom-right image of Figure 7.16 represents the final drawing.

Ring Toss Toy

In this demonstration, a ring toss toy (the left image of Figure 7.17) is our subject. A ring, or donut-shaped object, has two circles. So, we need to draw (at least) two ovals for each ring. In this case, three rings are placed facing in different directions. Therefore, each ring must be processed individually for information about its axis direction and proportion.

Again, you may find that many shape techniques are applicable for this drawing. Virtual bones, grouped graphical structures, and curved polygons are useful in this case. The center-left image of Figure 7.17 shows you a virtual bone for the body, a curved polygon for all three rings grouped together, and a rectangle for the base. A large pentagon shape bounds all of these structures.

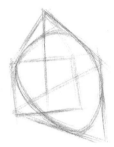

Figure 7.17

Ring toss toy (left), starting with overall shapes (center left), sketching all major structures (center right), and the final drawing (right)

The next step is to determine the structure of the ovals and cone body. As shown earlier, we need to decide the direction that each oval is facing. These directions will be the minor axes of the ovals for the drawing. In addition, the three rings are inside the curved polygon sketched in the previous step. The center-right image of Figure 7.17 shows what you can expect to achieve.

The final step is pretty simple if you have all of the structures placed in the right locations. However, if only two circles are drawn for each ring, the result will be very cartoonish. In order to make the rings feel more 3D, we have to add some textures to reflect the depth information inside each ring. You saw how an apple could be drawn using such reflection maps earlier in this chapter. The same technique is used here. The rightmost image of Figure 7.17 is the drawing that results.

Fruit

This demonstration shows you how to draw a shadow map and textures to boost the depth of simple objects. In the scene, a honeydew melon, two pears, and two apples are placed in direct sunlight, as shown in Figure 7.18. This is an ideal scene for using a shadow map because there are strong cast shadows everywhere.

Because there are several small, round objects and some cast shadows between them, it is pretty easy to group them to create large shapes. The top-left image of Figure 7.19 is where you will start. It contains two little, curved polygons. The polygons do not have to be drawn as accurately, for example, as when you are drawing human faces. They are just used to mark the overall structure at this point.

Figure 7.18

Figure 7.18

A grouping of fruit in direct sunlight

In the next step, further portioning is carried out. Ovals are sketched for each piece of fruit. To secure their sizes, we use reference lines, as you can see in the top-right image of Figure 7.19. Because these are randomly positioned pieces of fruit, sketching the ovals should not take up as much time as it did when you drew the camera lens. The axes information is not that critical here.

Figure 7.19

A fruit scene (top left), starting with a couple of curved polygons (top right), sketching all of the major structures (bottom left), and the final drawing (bottom right)

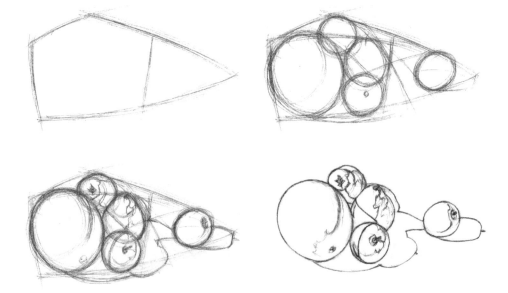

Next, we loosely place shadows and reflections on each object. It is a fairly easy job, because most of them are small-scaled objects. You should pay attention to the continuity of the cast shadows. When a large object casts a shadow on multiple objects nearby, the cast shadow line will run continuously from one object to another. If such continuity is broken in a drawing, the broken cast shadow may give viewers the wrong impression of the spatial relationship between objects.

When you sketch reflection patterns, primarily core shadows, just mark them loosely, because they don't have the same sharp boundary lines as do the cast shadows. The bottom-left image of Figure 7.19 shows the results of this step.

The last step is to finalize your lines. Because core shadows are thick, you should draw their boundaries a little irregularly. Otherwise, they will look like cast shadows. The bottom-right image of Figure 7.19 is the finished work.

Bath Faucet and Metal Shower Hose

This demonstration shows you how to use shadow maps or their variations for increasing the sense of 3D depth in a line-sketch drawing. A fairly complicated faucet and hose combination are presented in Figure 7.20. The subject is made of shiny metal, and you can see many reflections in the faucet from the surrounding environment. If you draw the faucet and accessories without such reflections, the result will be pretty flat and boring. Thus, it is a good idea to use the shadow map technique to express the reflections, just as we did in the previous fruit grouping demonstration.

Figure 7.20

Bath faucet and metal shower hose

You can use one of several techniques to get started. Beginning with a curved polygon is a good choice. A virtual skeleton also works well with the narrow hose structures. Feel free to use different techniques, as long as they help you arrange shapes on the paper efficiently and accurately. The top left image of Figure 7.21 is a simple start using a few curved lines.

The next step is to arrange the major structures inside the curved polygon that you have already sketched. When you arrange the objects in this step, focus on the major pipes and their relative sizes. Reference lines as well as the use of negative space are good techniques here. The top right image of Figure 7.21 shows the sketch you may have at this point.

Adding detailed structures, including reflections, is what you need to do next. There are some simple ovals in the scene. All of them face either vertical or horizontal directions. So, it is easy to set up the axes. However, you need to keep an eye on their proportions. All ovals facing up (in a vertical direction) should have the same proportions. So do the ovals facing horizontally. Some major reflections are sketched loosely to indicate their positions. The bottom left image of Figure 7.21 shows the results of this step.

The final stage is to draw nice, clean lines for the final drawing. Nothing needs to be added except the reflections. For a shiny metal object, the reflected images are usually narrow, smooth, and sharp. They are different from the core shadows. The bottom right image of Figure 7.21 displays the completed drawing.

Figure 7.21

A faucet system (top left), starting with curved polygons (top right), arranging major structures (bottom left), and the final drawing (bottom right)

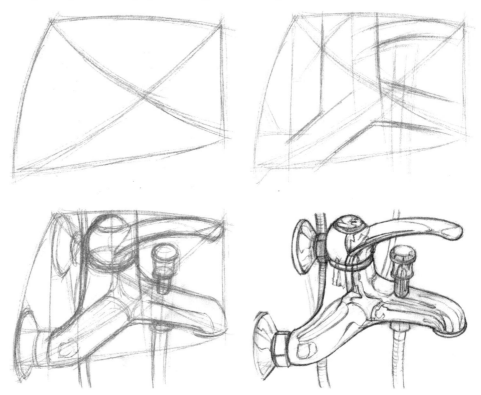

Yosemite National Park Scene

In outdoor drawing, you will observe that vertical and horizontal patterns frequently appear. At the same time, most natural objects are too complicated to extract their ministructures accurately. In such scenarios, it is easier to use rhythms for arranging the overall pictures before adding details.

The top left image of Figure 7.22 is a scene from Yosemite National Park. There is a big dead tree in the foreground, some trees in the middle range, and a mountain in the background. The vertical trees and horizontal patterns are useful for quickly laying out the drawing. The top right image of Figure 7.22 is one such example. In this image, a few horizontal lines are used to sketch the blocks of grass, the trees, and the mountain. The dead tree is also sketched in roughly.

Figure 7.22

A scene from Yosemite National Park (top left), using rhythm for a quick partitioning (top right), sketching structures roughly (bottom left), and the final drawing (bottom right)

The next image shows how the major structures are added. We determine the size of the foreground tree, place trees in the middle, and refine the outline of the mountain. After this step, the drawing is subdivided into small zones so that you just need to work on each area separately. The bottom right image of Figure 7.22 is the completed drawing.

Summary

In this chapter, you learned some new advanced techniques for drawing complicated scenes. So far, you have learned many techniques to assist you in using the ABC method. The demonstrations have covered almost everything up to this point—well, except for human figures. Surely you can now apply the ABC method to drawing the human body. However, if you want to draw the human body accurately, some additional techniques will be necessary. The next chapter presents these additional techniques.

Before you move on to the next chapter, however, please take some time to do the following exercises and reinforce the new techniques you just learned.

Exercises

CURVED TRIANGLES AND POLYGONS

1. Find five random scenes or photos, and identify curved triangles and polygons. Draw them on paper as a way to control structures quickly. You can use different selections for the same scene. Look at the results and ask yourself, which one is better and why?

SHADOW MAPS

2. Take a close-up photo of some objects under direct sunlight. Make sure that they have clearly defined shadows. Draw the objects by using shadow maps. (Don't render them.)

OVALS

3. Find five or more different-sized cans. Place them on a table so that they face random directions. Draw them from different angles. Pay close attention to the ovals.

4. Get several plastic bottles and fill them with different amounts of water. Place these bottles in front of you and draw them. Make sure that the water levels are drawn correctly.

RHYTHMS

5. Practice using rhythms with at least five landscapes. It's better to try different ones such as trees, gardens, buildings, and so on.

TRADE-OFF BETWEEN ACCURACY AND SPEED

6. Draw five landscape scenes that have various objects such as trees, rocks, buildings, rivers, etc. Focus on your interested parts and simplify or ignore non-interested areas.

CHAPTER 8

Using Special Techniques for Drawing Human Bodies

Art demands constant observation. — VINCENT VAN GOGH (1853–1890), DUTCH PAINTER

Drawing human figures is probably the most challenging task in learning to draw. The complicated movable structures of the human body create hundreds of distinct poses. Considering different viewing angles, body sizes, and costumes, a human figure presents us with an unlimited number of dynamic images.

Although most of us love drawing people starting from the day we first learn to draw, mastering the real skill of drawing human characters remains a difficult task.

To be good at drawing human figures, you really have to understand and be familiar with the detailed parts of the human body. Usually, a class in anatomy is necessary. In addition, you need lots of practice drawing people from real life.

The subject of figure drawing is so important that many books have been published on teaching artists how to draw people. I have no intention of teaching you everything about drawing people in this single chapter. Instead, you will be shown various techniques for drawing people that work with the ABC method. These useful tips will help you to draw complicated portraits and quick life sketches by integrating human anatomical knowledge with the techniques covered in the preceding chapters. To help you avoid the use of bad practices, this chapter also analyzes some inefficient approaches and common mistakes. As usual, various demonstrations are provided with explanations for easy understanding and follow-up exercises.

The following topics are covered in this chapter:

- General techniques for handling human body structures

- Tips for drawing faces

- Quick sketching techniques

General Tips

A human body is a complicated system that consists of over 200 bones and more than 600 muscles, according to Sarah Simblet's *Anatomy for the Artist* (Dorling Kindersley, 2001). As such, anatomy is a standard core-class in all professional art training. Without a good understanding of the human skeleton and muscle organization, an artist can hardly do a good job drawing a human figure realistically.

However, learning anatomy is just one step toward mastering figure drawing. Despite its usefulness, anatomical knowledge does not automatically give you the ability to put structures down on paper efficiently. It is your skill in shape management that turns the particular knowledge into real artwork. This section presents several techniques to help you draw the human body by using the ABC method. You may have seen some of these techniques elsewhere, perhaps in one of the numerous books published on drawing people, but you will learn how these tips work with the new approaches introduced in this book.

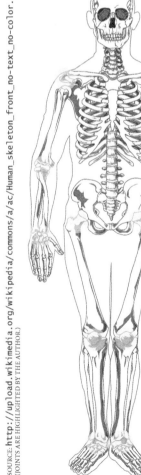

Figure 8.1

A human skeleton with major joints highlighted (front view)

SOURCE: http://upload.wikimedia.org/wikipedia/commons/a/ac/Human_skeleton_front_no-text_no-color.svg (JOINTS ARE HIGHLIGHTED BY THE AUTHOR.)

Tip 1: Using Joints and Landmarks as Key Points

One major feature of the ABC method is using key points to create and control graphical structures. Good key points will enable you to set up useful reference lines and construct simple but powerful triangles or polygons that approximate the original objects. Usually, identifying and selecting such points is based on your understanding of the target subject.

In figure drawing, our target is the highly complex human body. The human skeletal system (see Figure 8.1) can be divided into six parts: head, body/torso, two arms, and two legs. The torso mainly contains the rib cage, the pelvis, and the connecting backbone. It is the centerpiece of the skeleton from which the other five parts extend. The torso has fairly limited flexibility, and it can bend and twist only at certain angles, while the arms and legs have a much wider range of mobility. The joints in the arms and legs provide these parts with a great deal of freedom to move, rotate, and twist, even though the bones themselves are nondeformable, solid structures. With the preceding quick analysis, it is not hard for artists to figure out various ways that help in drawing the human body. One of them is using joints and landmarks. *Joints* are the connecting points between two adjacent bones inside the body, while a landmark is an important spot on the surface of the human body, typically at the place where different muscles meet.

Please be aware that both joints and landmarks may not be visible in a particular setting. So, you need to be familiar with some basic structures of the human body before you can identify and use these points. Some major joints are highlighted in Figure 8.1. These important points are extremely powerful in controlling body parts and are easy to find. You should always consider them as the key points in your drawing. Other joints, such as those in the fingers and toes, are not as influential to the whole body pose and therefore are not marked.

Usually, muscles have convex shapes, but there will be some concave spots where muscles meet. Such points are referred to as *landmarks* for the convenience of allocating muscles. Figure 8.2 shows some important landmarks on the body. The drawback of using landmarks is that you cannot see most of them on a clothed person. Therefore, unless you draw a nude model, the power of landmarks is limited.

Figure 8.2

Muscles in the human body and some landmarks

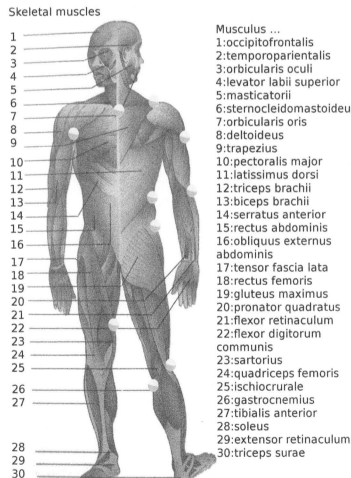

Skeletal muscles

1
2
3
4
5
6
7
8
9
10
11
12
13
14
15
16
17
18
19
20
21
22
23
24
25
26
27
28
29
30

Musculus ...
1:occipitofrontalis
2:temporoparientalis
3:orbicularis oculi
4:levator labii superior
5:masticatorii
6:sternocleidomastoideus
7:orbicularis oris
8:deltoideus
9:trapezius
10:pectoralis major
11:latissimus dorsi
12:triceps brachii
13:biceps brachii
14:serratus anterior
15:rectus abdominis
16:obliquus externus abdominis
17:tensor fascia lata
18:rectus femoris
19:gluteus maximus
20:pronator quadratus
21:flexor retinaculum
22:flexor digitorum communis
23:sartorius
24:quadriceps femoris
25:ischiocrurale
26:gastrocnemius
27:tibialis anterior
28:soleus
29:extensor retinaculum
30:triceps surae

SOURCE: http://en.wikipedia.org/wiki/File:Skeletal_muscles_homo_sapiens.jpg (LANDMARKS ARE HIGHLIGHTED BY THE AUTHOR.)

Figure 8.3 is a demonstration of the tips in this section. The top-left image is Michelangelo's painting *Isaiah*. The body of Isaiah is mainly covered, so you probably cannot use landmarks. But you can easily find the locations of the major joints, such as the elbows and knees. Therefore, a couple of simple curved polygons based on the visible joints are placed on paper, as shown in the center image. The head area is represented by a curved triangle. The clothing is simplified to a few basic curves. They serve as reference lines to connect the other polygons. A centerline for the body is drawn to mark the pose of the character as well as to indicate the position of the neck and head. As usual, multiple reference lines are used to ensure the relationship between the polygons on paper (see the top-center image of Figure 8.3). The rest of the process is pretty similar to the demonstrations from previous chapters. After you get these coarse-resolution polygons, the next step is to refine them and bring in the smaller-scaled structures. The head is represented by a simple oval, the arms and legs are drawn as rectangles, and so forth. The top-right image of Figure 8.3 shows the results of this step.

Figure 8.3

Isaiah (top left), initial polygons based on joints (top center), refined structures (top right), arranged facial features (bottom left), refinement of all detailed structures (bottom center), and the final drawing (bottom right)

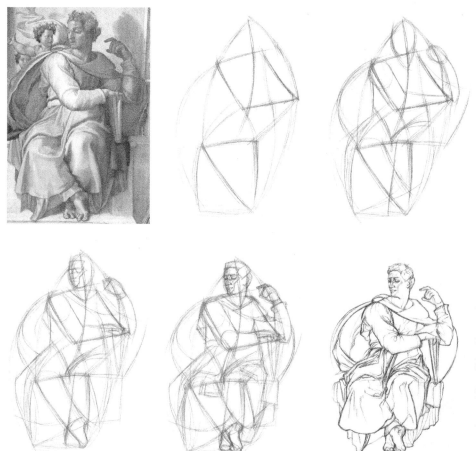

SOURCE: http://it.wikipedia.org/wiki/File:Jesaja_(Michelangelo).jpg

In the bottom-left image of Figure 8.3, facial features are arranged with a few additional lines. You will learn how to draw them in detail in the next section. The bottom-center image is what the drawing looks like if all structures are placed correctly. After you confirm that there are no major or obvious errors, you can add finishing lines for the whole picture, as shown in the bottom-right image of Figure 8.3.

Tip 2: Using Big Shapes for Measurement

In the previous chapters, you learned various methods for extracting and arranging big shapes from the target subjects. You always start by drawing the large structures first and then go down to the smaller ones. When you draw people, this fundamental principle remains the same. Many people tend to draw small structures, such as the head, and then use the head as the basic measurement unit to control the scale and positioning of the other body parts. The length relationship between the head and the other body parts is an essential part of anatomy. The size of the head is a good *static* reference in general, but it is not necessarily the best one for drawing *dynamic* figures. I've observed many art students lose control when drawing people if the model's head was foreshortened or even hidden.

Instead, you should find large dynamic structures and use them as a basis on which to build a drawing. You don't need to "measure" how many big structures a torso is, *per se*. The way we use structures hierarchically actually treats the top-level shapes, or large shapes, as measuring references for the whole picture. When you do that, you never lose your "measurement tool," and you never need to use a pencil to measure head and body sizes as traditional methods suggest.

Typically, you can find the following big structures quickly: a rectangle of the body (torso), triangles of bended arms and legs, a triangle from the top of the head to the shoulders, grouped structures of the body with arms or legs, and large pieces of clothing. If you are able to identify and arrange these big blocks, you'll have a very good overall structure of the subject. The top-center image of Figure 8.3 demonstrates some of these structures.

Tip 3: Using Centerline and Motion Flow Lines

Beside joints and landmarks, several lines are available to help you capture a pose. The *centerline* of the body is one of them. The line starts at the bottom center of the neck (the spot between the two clavicles), goes through the navel, and ends at the pubis. It is like an "axis" for the torso. Because of the bending and twisting of a body, such a centerline is typically curved. You can see the centerline in the left-center image of Figure 8.3.

ACTION LINES

In the animation field, animators commonly use action lines to express the body gesture of a character. Technically, *action lines* are simplified curves that represent the body, arms, and legs. Action lines are useful for designing a sequence of body gestures for cartoons. As you saw in the top-center image of Figure 8.3, the centerline and polygons already secure the body's gestures, so it is not necessary to use action lines here.

Unlike the centerline, which is a built-in part of a human body, many more dynamic lines are available to help you draw. In the ABC method, one major tactic of arranging objects is to use reference lines between objects, even though they may seem to be completely unrelated. When applied to figure drawing, you should "connect" various parts by motion flow lines. A *motion flow line* is a (curved) line that associates two moving parts so that they look like they are naturally linked. You can find such lines in the top-center image of Figure 8.3: a line connecting the left arm with the left foot, lines joining the top of the head to the left hand and to the right shoulder, and a line swooping from the right shoulder to the right knee joint. You should find many such dynamic connections in *any* pose. Using such lines creates flow between the arms and legs. More important, these lines make drawing much easier and more efficient.

Tip 4: Taking Advantage of Symmetry

Our body is symmetrical with respect to the centerline of the body. Symmetry is a major feature that we must use when drawing—from facial features to shoulders, arms, legs, and feet. When you draw, first make sure parts of a pair (for instance, the arms) have similar sizes. The same treatment should be applied to hands, legs, and feet. Inexperienced artists often draw unbalanced arms and legs. If you pay attention to symmetry, such mistakes are avoidable.

Besides the obvious symmetry of arms and legs, there are some not-so-obvious symmetry lines you can also use—for example, the *shoulder line*, which connects the two shoulders together even though they are blocked by the neck. If you don't use the shoulder line, you are likely to draw unbalanced shoulders. The foot line connects the two feet as if they are chained together. You will see an example of this in a later demonstration.

The four tips taught in this section are applicable to general figure drawing. You should use these tips when you draw human figures or animals, which share many similar anatomical structures with humans. Next we will go through another interesting and special topic—drawing human faces. Some tips associated with unique facial structures are presented.

Tips for Drawing Faces

It is obvious that drawing the human face is the hardest job in figure drawing. Drawing a person you know is even harder. There is an old Chinese saying: "It is easy to draw a ghost but hard to draw a person you know." When you illustrate a friend or a public figure, any small misalignment of facial features will immediately be noticeable and thus damage your portrait drawing. This is completely different from drawing a flower or a building. The accuracy requirement for managing structures is much higher in a portrait than for any other subject type.

All of the methods and tips you learned so far are still useful here. But there are some additional tips that can make you more efficient in controlling facial structures. You will learn about a few of them in this section.

Tip 5: Using Feature Lines for Layout

Many books talk about measurements of facial structures. Figure 8.4 is originally from Andrew Loomis's, *Drawing the Head & Hands* (Titan Books, 2011). I added some highlights and additional lines for the purpose of further studies in this section. The image shows various length and height relationships between the eyes, nose, mouth, ears, and so forth. Almost all artists use this kind of chart for figure drawing these days.

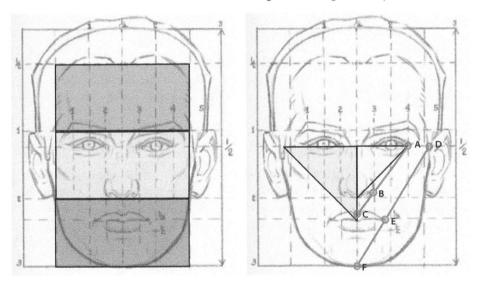

Figure 8.4

Static graphical structures in a human face

A face includes several major features: two eyes, two eyebrows, one nose, one mouth or two lips, and two ears. Among them, the eyes are the most important, so you should spend more time drawing the eyes correctly. If you draw a horizontal line at a particular feature, you will get a *feature line*. In a face, you can create the following important ones: the eyebrow line, the eye line, the nose line, the mouth line, the chin line, and the hair line. The centerline (axis) of a face is the only vertical line that goes though two features: the nose and mouth. All of these lines are on the surface of an egg-shaped 3D head. Therefore, they appear to be a little curved in a drawing.

These lines have some useful properties that fit for most people. Artists have used the following guidelines for a long time: the hair line, the eyebrow line, the nose line, and the chin line divide a face into three equal-height zones (marked by highlights on the left side of Figure 8.4). Additionally, eye width, nose width, and the space between the two eyes are the same.

These measurement relationships between features are extremely useful. However, others are often overlooked. Angular relationships between these features, for example, are also very helpful, especially when using the ABC method. The right side of Figure 8.4 indicates some of these important angular relationships.

In the right side of the image, two isosceles right triangles are placed. Both triangles align with the eye line and the center line. The longest edge of the larger triangle runs from the center of the mouth to the widest point of the face on the eye line. The smaller triangle's longest edge connects the outside point of an eye and the bottom of the nose. These triangles indicate some interesting size relationships between length and width of the features: the nose length is about one and a half of an eye's width. The distance between the eye line to the mouth line is about half of the face width. Additionally, two diagonal lines are drawn in the image to show some useful coincidences as indicated by the six points A through F.

The following is a demonstration of the tips discussed in this section.

JFK

The top-left image of Figure 8.5 is a portrait of John F. Kennedy, the 35th president of the United States. This famous public figure was purposely selected to challenge your drawing skills. The top-center image is the initial sketch on paper. It contains a simple oval for the head and a rectangle for the area of the face. A centerline is set up in the middle because this is a front-view portrait. A hair line is placed at the top of the rectangle. An eyebrow line and a nose line are placed in the middle of the rectangle. The bottom of the rectangle is the chin line. The cross lines in the rectangle are reference lines for controlling the proportion of the rectangle. Because this portrait is angled from below, the distance between the nose line and the chin line is slightly longer, while the distance between the hair line and the eyebrow line is slightly shortened.

Arranging the position of the eyes and nose is critical to the overall layout, so please take some extra time to confirm these relationships. Feel free to create more reference lines as needed. Untrained people often start drawing the eyes before making a global layout. This is a bad habit, and it usually results in a poor relationship among facial features.

We will come back to this demo after you read the next tip.

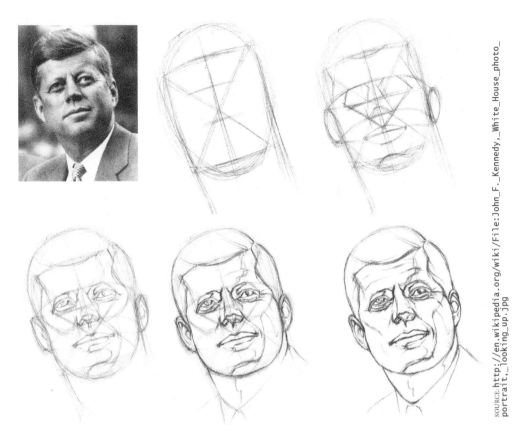

SOURCE: http://en.wikipedia.org/wiki/File:John_F._Kennedy,_White_House_photo_portrait,_looking_up.jpg

Figure 8.5

A picture of JFK (top left), initial polygons and feature lines (top center), polygons for eyes and eye-nose triangle (top right), arranged facial structures detail (bottom left), all detailed structures drawn (bottom center), and some minor problems fixed (bottom right)

Tip 6: Controlling Sizes with Polygons

After allocating the positions for the eyes and nose, you need to determine the size of the features. It is commonly assumed that the eyes and nose have the same width. But this assumption is only for sizes in the horizontal direction. In order to control the shapes of the eyes and nose, we need some extra help.

Using a sunglasses shape for the eyes is an efficient technique employed by many artists. Drawing a pair of ovals to cover the area of the eyes will allow you to control this important region quickly. In the top-right image of Figure 8.5, you will see a pair of polygons over the eyes. I prefer polygons because they are easier to duplicate than ovals. Most beginners tend to draw long noses. But the nose line effectively prevents this mistake.

The mouth line is above the middle point between the nose and the chin. The two end points of the mouth are roughly beneath the middle of each eye. Unlike the eyes and nose, the mouth is flexible depending on different emotions. So when you draw the mouth, you need to pay attention to its width with respect to the nose, which is not flexible.

At this point, you just need to sketch the overall shape of the mouth without detailed lip lines. In the right side of Figure 8.4, we see that the points A, B, and C are on a line in general. So, I used this property to confirm the relationship between the ends of the eyes, the sides of the nose, and the top-center point of the upper lip. The ears are positioned between the eyebrow line and the nose line. The top-right image of Figure 8.5 shows this.

This demonstration is continued in the next tip.

Tip 7: Drawing a 3D Nose and Using Wrinkles

Unlike the eyes and mouth, the nose has a considerable height. In order to express its 3D form, it is a good idea to draw a triangle at the bottom of the nose. The top-right image of Figure 8.5 shows such a drawing. For a better understanding, Figure 8.6 provides some extra help. The left side of Figure 8.6 is an example of a poor drawing in which the nose seems to be flat. The right side of Figure 8.6 makes the nose much more multidimensional.

Figure 8.6

Bad and good examples of drawing a nose

It is well known that drawing old men is much easier than drawing children and young women. Wrinkles on an old man's face are very valuable reference lines that can assist your drawing. In the bottom-left image of Figure 8.5, you will see some of them, but not many. Also, in this image, all structures are sketched. The next step is to replace the sketch lines with fine lines (see the bottom-center image of Figure 8.5).

These tips and the ABC method will improve your ability to draw structures. But it is by no means a guarantee that you will not make mistakes when you actually implement these approaches. So, it is always helpful to take a final look at your artwork and fix any minor issues. This is exactly the case for the results I have obtained so far. The left ear is too low, and the neck is too thick in the drawing, so these kinds of errors are fixed in the final version displayed in the bottom-right image of Figure 8.5.

Tip 8: A General Face-Drawing Process

If you are a beginner, you may feel there are too many rules and tips for drawing a face. Indeed, the measurements addressed earlier are *not* forged in stone—they are just for the ideal face in *front view*. Use them only as a guide—everyone will have slightly different measurements. Furthermore, the eyebrow line, the mouth line, and the chin line are *flexible* with emotions, while the eye line, nose line, and hair line are not. The following points clear up the usage of these rules:

- The three-zone vertical partition still works for nonfrontal-view faces. However, the top zone will be shortened and the bottom will be stretched if the head is looking up. The relationship will be swapped if the head is looking down.

- The centerline is usually not quite in the center of the face for a normal face position. But it is still a useful tool to divide the face into two half-faces in a pose with both eyes visible.

- The following three points are still on a line in general: side point of the eye, side point of the nose, and center of the upper lip.

- Ear size is controlled by the eyebrow line and nose line in all poses. But these two lines are curved because they are on the surface of a sphere.

- The eye vs. nose width relationship does not hold in general. So, don't use it as a rule to draw a normal face.

To provide you with additional help in drawing a typical face, here is a step-by-step procedure that I recommend you follow:

1. Draw an oval to represent the head and a rectangle to represent the face. Partition the rectangle into three zones horizontally by inserting the eyebrow line and the nose line. Place the centerline to divide the face into two parts in the vertical direction.

2. Draw a pair of sunglasses or polygons to cover the eyes. Draw a triangle for the bottom of the nose. Draw an outline for the mouth in the middle area between the nose and the chin. Extend the eyebrow line and nose line to determine the size and position of the ears. Use the side point of an eye, the side point of the nose, and the midpoint of the upper lip to confirm a linear relationship.

3. Sketch in detail for all of the facial features. The eyebrows will be on the top boundaries of the sunglasses, and the eyes will be inside the glass shapes. Use dynamic reference lines to secure spatial relationships. Any general techniques introduced in the preceding chapters are applicable to faces.

4. Finalize your lines.

Figure 8.7 shows an example of these four basic steps.

Once again, all these tips are designed to provide extra help in addition to the general dynamic reference strategy used in the ABC method. If you are lost when using these unique rules, always turn to reference lines between the different features for the particular pose. It always works.

Figure 8.7

Step 1 (left), step 2 (center left), step 3 (center right), and step 4 (right)

Drawing portraits requires a higher degree of accuracy, and you probably will spend a long time, from half an hour to several hours, on a single drawing. There is an opposite side to practice: the quick sketch, which uses short time frames for capturing figure poses. This will be our next topic.

Tips for Quick Life Sketches

Working under a time constraint is always a challenging and sometimes a frustrating task for entry-level artists. A *quick sketch* is a popular drawing practice that tries to capture a subject in a small amount of time. In professional art schools, the time for a quick sketch is typically set between 1 and 5 minutes for both clothed and nude models. The goal of such training is to teach artists to record the most essential parts of various poses so that artists can design and create characters in the future. When extracting graphical information and duplicating shapes on paper in a very short time, the efficiency of your drawing method is essential.

Generally speaking, you are not allowed to waste any time whatsoever when you do a quick sketch. You need to keep your pencil moving on the paper, and every single pencil stroke should be productive and constructive. This fits perfectly with the principle of the ABC method, which focuses on efficiency. Because quick sketching is an advanced method, you are expected to use shapes directly instead of using key points.

Quick sketching can be considered an engineering process for achieving maximum visual product within a time limit. To do so, you have to trade off accuracy for drawing speed. In this section, I will share with you some techniques that work with the ABC method in order to achieve high efficiency. I have used them for the past few years in the quick sketching of life models.

Tip 9: Using Simple Shapes for Quick Layout

Figure 8.8

A 2-minute life figure drawing

Because you don't have much time in quick sketching, you need to use a small number of simple and big shapes to represent figures. The good news is that you can always find such shapes in a dynamic figure. Because of the time limits, the ABC method is simplified into two major steps: construct big shapes and add final detail immediately. You don't have time to create various structures in short poses. I typically spend 10–20 seconds for the first step, and then I use the rest of the time for drawing and rendering details.

Figure 8.8 is a 2-minute quick sketch of a life figure. To get the maximum visual effect, I use an elongated charcoal pencil for fast rendering. Because rendering is not covered in this book, I will show you how to do a quick line-drawing with a regular pencil.

The left image of Figure 8.9 is done in a 5-minute pose. Surely you can identify several simple shapes from this pose quickly. The center image of Figure 8.9 shows a few that I re-created for this chapter. You should not spend more than 30 seconds putting down these lines on paper. Don't chase after high accuracy here, because we forego accuracy for faster speed. After this step, you have the rest of the time to draw in detail. The right image of Figure 8.9 is what I get by sketching out major features.

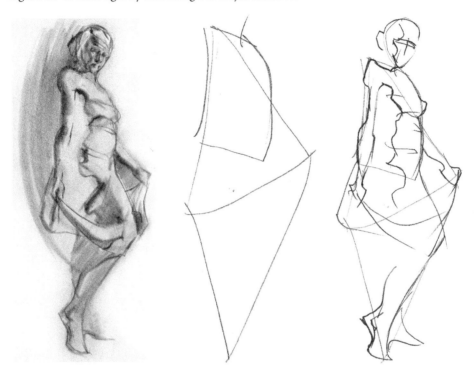

Figure 8.9

A 5-minute quick sketching (left), simple shapes re-created (center), and a line drawing (right)

There are several common mistakes I've observed in students when they learn quick sketching. One problem is that they start from detail, just as in the contour-line method. Typically, the drawing deteriorated to poor structures quickly. The second mistake is illustrating body parts as 3D forms—for instance, using cylinders to draw arms and legs. Such treatments are good for understanding the 3D structures of a human body in anatomy class, but in a quick-sketch drawing, this method will waste time and slow down the drawing process. A third mistake is to draw stick figures. Frankly speaking, a stick figure is a very efficient way to capture a human figure. However, a stick figure is a simplified skeleton and contains no information about muscles. This type of drawing is too simple and inartistic to be used as a form of quick sketching for professional artists.

STICK FIGURES

A *stick figure* drawing is a simple and symbolic way to draw figures. It contains a few sticks to represent the torso, arms, and legs. A stick figure can capture the essential gesture of a body pose with minimum effort.

A stick figure is a perfect method for beginners and children who want to represent a human figure. It is also a good tool for artists to design character poses for animations quickly.

Tip 10: Using Core Shadows

In Chapter 7, "Using Advanced Techniques," you learned a little bit about core shadows for boosting the 3D effects of pieces of fruit. Despite a simple (thick) line, a core shadow can express the 3D structure underneath. A curved core shadow indicates a round object, while a straight line hints at a flat structure. Unlike a stick figure, a core shadow is dynamic, depending on the light source. So, a core shadow is more artistic and more interesting than a straight line.

The left side of Figure 8.10 is a ballet dancer under strong lights on a stage. The strong core shadows in the body, arms, and legs clearly show us the 3D volume of the structures. Usually, you need a thick pencil to express the core shadows because they are not thin lines. The right image of Figure 8.10 is a quick sketch with a thick Expo marker.

Figure 8.10

Core shadows in a dancer (left) and a quick sketch using core shadows (right)

I tend to call core shadows *dynamic skeletons*, because core shadows appear at each body part (when there are strong lights on both sides). These core shadows connected naturally as a beautiful "skeleton," as you can see in Figure 8.10. Unlike a traditional skeleton or stick figures, this "skeleton" carries musculature information, so it is a very efficient way to express 3D structures.

Although we don't address shadows in this book, there are some shadow-based tricks that are useful for quick sketching. Shadow maps are clearly one of them that you already learned about in Chapter 7. Another technique is to use shadow to hint at smaller features, such as the eyes, nose, and mouth, in a simple way without spending too much time drawing detail. Drawing the dark side of an object can tell viewers about a structure implicitly. Figure 8.11 shows two drawings in which simple shadows are drawn to illustrate facial features. Using this method, you don't have to draw all the outlines of an object. It will save you time and increase your efficiency. The drawing results are also interesting.

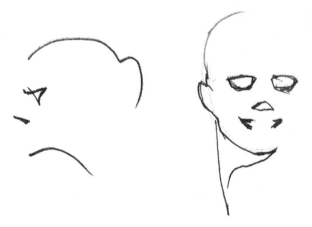

Tip 11: Focusing on the Torso

Many beginners spend a lot of time drawing the head and face in life drawings. In a short-time drawing, this will take up most of your time because the facial features are so complicated. Instead, you should focus on the torso, which is the centerpiece of a body and its gestures. By bending and twisting, the torso sends a strong visual message to viewers about what the body is doing.

A torso can be approximated by two ovals or a bent rectangle, and you can quickly attach arms and legs to the torso afterward. Figure 8.12 shows examples of both cases. You will see that only a few lines are used to draw these poses.

Tip 12: Drawing Selectively

Quick sketching is a time-constrained activity. You don't have to draw everything you see about the figure. Instead, you should concentrate on the major parts in which you are interested so that you can finish in the limited amount of time you have. Most of the time, the head is not important at all, and you can symbolically draw an oval or even ignore it. Another commonly undrawn area is the dark side of a model. You can simply leave it blank (see the left image of Figure 8.9 earlier) or draw it as a big shadow area.

Figure 8.13 shows some examples of 2-minute life drawings I made. You will see that I ignored lots of parts on purpose and thus saved time for rendering.

Figure 8.12

A torso as a rectangle (left) and a torso as two ovals (right)

The 12 tips presented in this chapter will enable you to draw faster and better. You need to practice these tips in order to add them to your drawing skills. Be aware that these tips are just a small part of the knowledge you'll need for figure drawing. The most valuable knowledge comes from the study of human anatomy, and you should take a class in this subject when you have chance.

To help you master the techniques addressed in this section, more demonstrations are provided in the next section.

Figure 8.13

Some samples of 2-minute life drawings

Demonstrations

In this section, you will have additional opportunities to see how the ABC method works with the dozen tips discussed earlier. Follow along, and practice as you read through this section.

Woman

The top-left image of Figure 8.14 is a photo of woman sitting by a wall. We can clearly see the joints in her arms and the overall shape of her body. Therefore, it is pretty easy to start with a couple of lines to lock the torso and arms. The head is also restricted by a curved triangle, as you can see in the top-center image of Figure 8.14.

Figure 8.14

A picture of a woman (top left), initial lines (top center), locking major structures (top right), refining face and hands (bottom left), drawing all detailed structures (bottom center), and the final artwork (bottom right)

Next, a few shapes are added to allocate some major structures, such as the head, arms, and hands. When you sketch the arms, make sure their sizes are similar. The top-right image of Figure 8.14 is what you should get.

The bottom-left image of Figure 8.14 explains what you need to do next: refining the structures, especially the facial area and the hands. You will see that multiple feature lines and sunglasses are drawn in to secure the positions of these important features. When you refine the hands, don't add the details of the fingers. Instead, divide the hand into a palm and a finger area, as you see in the demo.

You should have all kinds of major structures at this point, so it is time to draw in the details such as the fingers, facial features, and wrinkles in the clothing. This is the last sketch you'll draw before the final lines are added. The bottom-center image of Figure 8.14 is the version ready to be finalized, and the bottom-right image is the final render of this demonstration.

Rodin's Sculpture *The Thinker*

I strongly suggest that you draw real models if you have chance. Although you will use exactly the same drawing methods for real models as you do for photos, you have to project a 3D figure onto the picture plane. This process needs some practice despite its simplicity. Street sculptures are good alternatives for practicing observational figure drawing. These "figures" don't move while you draw them, and you can come back again and again.

In this demonstration, a street sculpture *The Thinker* is our subject. The top-left image of Figure 8.15 is the picture of Auguste Rodin's famous work. The angle of this photo allows you to easily find many joints of the body. These joints are good for creating polygons that subdivide the figure into several parts (see the top-center image).

In this sitting pose, the arms and legs dominate the whole scene, so your focus should be on managing these parts. The top-right image of Figure 8.15 shows how the arms and legs are placed by using multiple, grouped graphical structures. When you have multiple objects/parts gathering in the same area, grouping them is an effective way to control their orientations simultaneously.

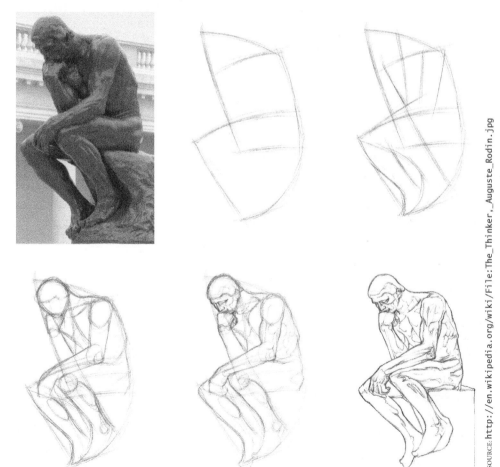

Figure 8.15

A picture of *The Thinker* (top left), initial polygons (top center), sketching arms and legs (top right), arranging detailed structures (bottom left), drawing face and muscles (bottom center), and the final artwork (bottom right)

SOURCE: http://en.wikipedia.org/wiki/File:The_Thinker,_Auguste_Rodin.jpg

In the next image, you see that I sketched the head and a few muscles in the arms and the legs. Further detail is shown in the bottom-center image of Figure 8.15. When you sketch a nude figure, anatomical knowledge plays an important role when drawing the muscles. Getting familiar with muscle shapes and locations can greatly improve your figure drawing ability. In the bottom-right image of Figure 8.15, the drawing is finished by illustrating the many muscles that span the body. Without these muscle lines, the picture will look flat and less interesting.

Einstein

In this demonstration, we will draw Albert Einstein's portrait (see the top-left image of Figure 8.16). In this picture, Einstein's head is turned to the left; therefore the front-view facial measurement relationship does not work well here. Additionally, Einstein's facial features are different from those of an average person. For example, he has a big nose, thick eyebrows, and a mustache. As such, you need to explore more-dynamic structures in order to arrange his facial structures.

The top-center image is the initial polygon. It has a very simple rectangular shape for the face and a big curved quadrilateral for the whole head, including the puffy hair. Inside the face, the eyebrow line and nose line are added to divide the facial area. A slightly curved center line is also placed. A pair of ovals is used to cover both the eyes and nose, as shown in the top-right image of Figure 8.16.

Figure 8.16

A picture of Einstein (top left), initial polygons (top center), feature lines, sunglasses, and eye-nose triangle (top right), arranging detailed facial structures (bottom left), drawing all detailed structures (bottom center), and fixing some minor problems (bottom right)

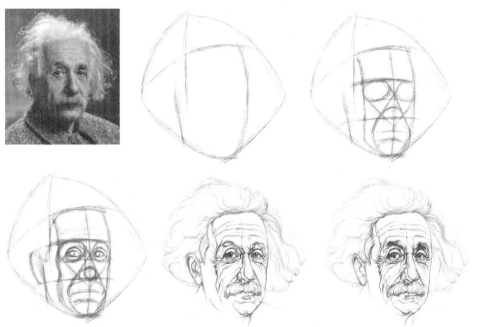

SOURCE: http://en.wikipedia.org/wiki/File:Albert_Einstein_Head.jpg

Sketching structures for the eyes, nose, and mustache is the next task. Spend more time on the eyes to ensure you can make them as accurate as possible. A pair of precisely drawn eyes is essential for a good portrait drawing. Use as many reference lines as you need. The bottom left image of Figure 8.16 is what you are expected to achieve. If you don't see any obvious mistakes at this step, you can add all the small details. You should take advantage of the wrinkles across his face. Aside from reference purposes, the wrinkles are real lines that represent skin structures and human aging. After you finish this step, you will have a pretty complete portrait of Einstein, as shown in the bottom-center image of Figure 8.16.

If you are not quite happy about the results, you are not alone. I see many minor problems in my drawing too. No drawing method can give you the accuracy of a photocopy. Although the ABC method provides us with some scientific tips on how to arrange structures, we still have limited hand-coordination ability. Big mistakes will rarely occur because of the various shape-control techniques employed, but minor mistakes are inevitable. Some problems are easy to fix, but others are structural problems and are thus harder to adjust. The bottom-right image of Figure 8.16 is the result of my attempt to fix some of these problems.

As discussed in Chapter 1, "Understanding the Relationship between Math and Art," hand-coordination ability can be improved via constant practice. However, this could be a slow process, and it is restricted by an unbreakable physical limitation.

Little Boy

As I mentioned earlier, old people have many more natural reference lines (wrinkles) than young ladies and children. Therefore, drawing a child or a woman is usually harder. In this demonstration, you will have a chance to draw a little boy from a photo to see the challenges.

The top-left image of Figure 8.17 is a photo of a little boy in an almost side view. Because of this angle, most static front-view relationships between features cannot be applied, except for the three equal zones formed by the eyebrow line and nose line. Additionally, unlike Einstein's photo, there is a big, blank area without any noticeable marker in the boy's face. Although these characteristics make your task harder, there is a positive side. The boy's head is fairly round. His major features are compressed into a small zone, so we can find many dynamic graphical structures.

The top-center image of Figure 8.17 is how you begin the process. A circle plus a triangle is a good approximation of the head shape. The feature lines are still visible here, and they divide the face into three zones. Make sure the bottom zone is a little bit bigger because of the subject's open mouth.

Adding structures is a process of using grouped graphical structures. You can see that the eyes, nose, and mouth form several different polygons, as sketched in the top-right image of Figure 8.17. The side hair line is used to control the location of the ear. The top-right image of Figure 8.17 shows you how these techniques are applied.

Figure 8.17

A picture of little boy (top left), initial circle, polygon, and feature lines (top center), polygons for eyes, nose, and mouth (top right), arranging detailed facial structures (bottom left), drawing all detailed structures (bottom center), and fixing some minor problems (bottom right)

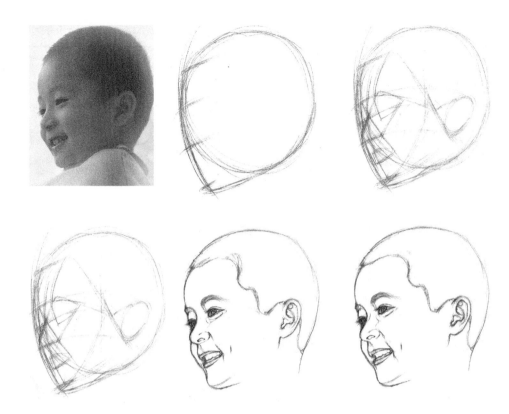

The next step is sketching the detailed structures. When adding small structures such as lips or the muscles below eyes, you should use and compare them with the established structures. The more references you use, the greater the chance to minimize drawing errors. These errors, which are caused by the limited ability to control your hands, are inevitable. However, they can be reduced, if not eliminated completely. The bottom-left image of Figure 8.17 is the result of this step.

You are probably eager to finalize all the detailed lines. If you don't see obvious errors, go ahead and do so. I got the bottom-center image when I replaced sketching lines with nice smooth curves. The result is fairly good, but you can still spot some mistakes if you pay very close attention to detailed parts. For example, the line on the top of the nose is not quite right. The hair line near the ear is also off. So, a quick fix is done in the bottom-right image of Figure 8.17.

More Life Drawing Samples

In this section, you will see some time-limited demonstrations—examples of short poses ranging from 1 minute to 5 minutes. Figure 8.18 contains five quick 1-minute sketches. For such a limited time, you usually need to capture the big shapes in few seconds and then spend the rest of the time adding details.

Figure 8.18
Five 1-minute quick sketches

Figure 8.19 displays some 2-minute quick sketches in different styles. Depending on the lighting, I usually use line-drawing for nonshadowed poses and do rendering if shadows are present.

Figure 8.19
Five 2-minute quick sketches

In most cases, I spend little or no time on facial features for 1-minute and 2-minute poses. However, 5-minute poses are different. I typically do both facial drawing as well as rendering. Figure 8.20 shows such examples.

Figure 8.20

Five 5-minute quick sketches

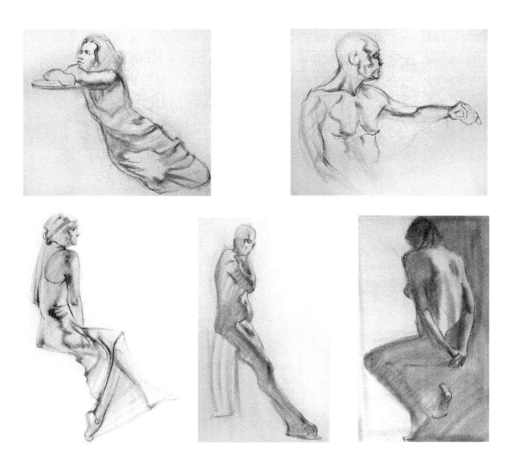

I hope you like the quick sketch samples provided here. Sketching under a time limit is a true test of drawing efficiency. You have to streamline the processes of extracting and arranging graphical information. In my experience, the ABC method allows an artist to grab and simplify interesting structures and reassemble them promptly on paper. The magic parallel-check technique avoids wasting a single second as compared to the pencil-measure method. The science of shapes shows its power for increasing drawing efficiency.

Summary

In this chapter, you learned a dozen of tips that are specially associated with drawing human bodies. This is just another example to prove that the better you know the drawing subject, the more spatial properties you can discover and thus the better you can draw. Many more properties exist for people in different races, gender, and ages. You need to find them by yourself to help your drawing.

As usual, you are expected to do exercises for this last chapter.

Exercises

JOINTS

1. Find five or more photos that contain some people in motion—for example, running, jumping, or diving. Identify the major joints of the target subject, and use the joints to form some interesting polygons and draw them on paper.

SIZE RELATIONSHIPS BETWEEN FACIAL FEATURES

2. Grab 10 random front-view face images from the Internet. For each of them, study the relationship between eye width, nose width, nose length, mouth width, and so on. Compare your observations with the theory expressed in Figure 8.4, and evaluate the accuracy of that theory.

FACE DRAWING PROCESS

3. Use tip 8 to duplicate at least five portraits of family members.

QUICK SKETCHES

4. Practice some quick sketches. If you don't have previous experience, try drawing family members or friends. Ask them to maintain some easy positions for 5 minutes or so. Don't try lengthy-held or strange poses because it may hurt their muscles or possibly cause injury. If you are an experienced artist, try quick sketches in a short time span (1–2 minutes) with the tips in this section.

KILL TIME BY QUICK SKETCHING

5. Make it a habit to draw whenever you have idle time. Bring a pocket sketchbook with you, and start to draw everything you see when you are waiting in restaurants, airports, and so on. Furniture, buildings, and people are all good subjects for observational drawing. Although it is a good way to kill time, it also improves your drawing skill on a daily basis.

Post-Test: Drawing Van Gogh

In the introduction of this book, you were asked to draw a portrait of Van Gogh as a way to record your current drawing skill prior to learning the theories and techniques presented in this book. To evaluate your progress after reading this book and doing all the exercises, you need to draw that same picture again, using the skills that you have acquired. Please go to the end of the introduction for detailed instructions. Make sure that you draw the portrait on the same-sized sheet of paper and complete it in approximately the same amount of time. After you are finished, compare your new drawing with your old one. If you truly follow the lessons in this book and have diligently completed the exercises, you should see a noticeable difference!

The degree of improvement will vary among individuals. But there is one big degree of progress common to all: everyone understands the simple process of drawing scientifically and that drawing is an activity of both sides of the brain.

Duplicating objects on paper is indeed an *engineering* task rather than an action of *feeling*. Basic math knowledge enables us to understand the properties of shapes and their behavior in 2D space. Beyond that, computer graphics principles bring us strategies to extract graphical information efficiently and to arrange shapes on paper constructively.

Thank you for taking this journey with me. I hope you enjoyed this book, even if you felt frustrated at times. Please remember that math and science are both needed to support high-performance drawing.

Index

Note to the Reader: Throughout this index **boldfaced** page numbers indicate primary discussions of a topic. *Italicized* page numbers indicate illustrations.